The Notion of Relevance in Information Science

Everybody knows what relevance is.

But, what is it really?

Synthesis Lectures on Information Concepts, Retrieval, and Services

Gary Marchionini, *University of North Carolina, Chapel Hill*

Synthesis Lectures on Information Concepts, Retrieval, and Services publishes short books on topics pertaining to information science and applications of technology to information discovery, production, distribution, and management. Potential topics include: data models, indexing theory and algorithms, classification, information architecture, information economics, privacy and identity, scholarly communication, bibliometrics and webometrics, personal information management, human information behavior, digital libraries, archives and preservation, cultural informatics, information retrieval evaluation, data fusion, relevance feedback, recommendation systems, question answering, natural language processing for retrieval, text summarization, multimedia retrieval, multilingual retrieval, and exploratory search.

The Notion of Relevance in Information Science: Everybody knows what relevance is. But, what is it really?
Tefko Saracevic

Dynamic Information Retrieval Modeling
Grace Hui Yang, Marc Sloan, Jun Wang

Learning from Multiple Social Networks
Liqiang Nie, Xuemeng Song, Tat-Seng Chua

Scholarly Collaboration on the Academic Social Web
Daqing He, Wei Jeng

Scalability Challenges in Web Search Engines
B. Barla Cambazoglu, Ricardo Baeza-Yates

Social Informatics Evolving
Pnina Fichman, Madelyn R. Sanfilippo, and Howard Rosenbaum

relevance
noun rel·e·vance \ˈre-lə-vən(t)s

Definition of *relevance*
Popularity: Top 30% of words

1. (a) relation to the matter at hand (b) practical and especially social applica-bility: pertinence <*giving relevance to college courses*>

2. the ability (as of an information retrieval system) to retrieve material that satisfies the needs of the user

Related to relevance:
Synonyms
applicability, bearing, connection, materiality, pertinence, relevancy
First known use of relevance: 1733

Meriam-Webster Dictionary
http://www.merriam-webster.com/dictionary/relevance

The Notion of Relevance in Information Science:
Everybody knows what relevance is. But, what is it really?
Tefko Saracevic

      ISBN: 978-3-031-01174-0   print
      ISBN: 978-3-031-02302-6   ebook

DOI 10.1007/978-3-031-02302-6

A Publication in the Springer series
SYNTHESIS LECTURES ON INFORMATION CONCEPTS, RETRIEVAL, AND SERVICES, #50
Series Editor: Gary Marchionini, University of North Carolina, Chapel Hill

Series ISSN 1947-945X Print   1947-9468 Electronic

The Notion of Relevance in Information Science

Everybody knows what relevance is.

But, what is it really?

Tefko Saracevic
Rutgers University

SYNTHESIS LECTURES ON INFORMATION CONCEPTS, RETRIEVAL, AND SERVICES #50

ABSTRACT

Everybody knows what relevance is. It is a "y'know" notion, concept, idea—no need to explain whatsoever. Searching for relevant information using information technology (IT) became a ubiquitous activity in contemporary information society. *Relevant* information means information that pertains to the matter or problem at hand—it is directly connected with effective communication. The purpose of this book is to trace the evolution and with it the history of thinking and research on relevance in information science and related fields from the human point of view. The objective is to synthesize what we have learned about relevance in several decades of investigation about the notion in information science. This book deals with how people deal with relevance—it does *not* cover how systems deal with relevance; it does *not* deal with algorithms. Spurred by advances in information retrieval (IR) and information systems of various kinds in handling of relevance, a number of basic questions are raised: *But what is relevance to start with? What are some of its properties and manifestations? How do people treat relevance? What affects relevance assessments? What are the effects of inconsistent human relevance judgments on tests of relative performance of different IR algorithms or approaches?* These general questions are discussed in detail.

KEYWORDS

relevance, information retrieval (IR), relevance behavior, relevance effects

Contents

Figures

Acknowledgments

Under its search box, Google Scholar has a cryptic command: "*Stand on the shoulders of giants.*" A few centuries ago, Isaac Newton, referring to Galileo and Kepler, said it better:

> "*If I have seen further [than certain other men] it is by standing upon the shoulders of giants*" (letter to Robert Hooke, February 5, 1675).

And a few centuries before that, in the 12th century, Bernard of Chartres (as reported by John of Salisbury) said it even better:

> "*We are like dwarfs sitting on the shoulders of giants; we see more things and more distant things than did they, not because our sight is keener nor because we are taller than they, but because they lift us up and add their giant stature to our height*" (Metalogicon, III, 4).

In that spirit, I owe a debt of gratitude to all authors included in the references. They did the hard work. I stood on their shoulders and saw further.

My heartfelt thanks to Gary Marchionini, the Editor of the Synthesis Lectures on Information Concepts, Retrieval, and Services. He suggested this work to me some years ago, and then over the years prodded the process gently toward completion, and made helpful comments along the way. It is my fault that I am late in producing it.

Special thanks to Diane Cerra, Executive Editor, Morgan & Claypool Publishers—she was not only encouraging when encouragement was needed, but also thoroughly and joyfully professional when professional help and guidance was required.

Thanks to Yuelin Li and Ying Zhang, my assistants at the time when this work begun, who tirelessly searched the literature for sources about relevance and then organized them. My colleagues at the School of Communication and Information, Rutgers University, provided a most hospitable framework for scholarly work and musings, and my students were a source of constant challenge, not only when I was there, but also now that I am retired as Distinguished Professor Emeritus. I am not only grateful, but also happy and proud to have worked and that I am still working in that environment.

From lifelong study of relevance, I learned a lot. I also learned how little I know.

Preface

Everybody knows what relevance is. *But, what is it really?* That is the subject of this book. Actually, the book is a treatise about thinking and research on the subject of relevance in the field of information science and related fields.

Relevance is an intensely human notion. It is a people thing. Relevant information is a human assessment, a judgment, a drawing of connection between given information and a given context or problem at hand.

One more thing: like all human notions, relevance is messy. The book tries to make our understanding of relevance less messy.

Contemporary information technology tries to assist people in obtaining relevant information. A never-ending succession of systems, processes, algorithms, and displays are being devised to do so. Every one of them is assuming something about relevance—what makes relevant information relevant—and it goes from there—actually, their coverage and algorithms go from there.

Yet, what is "relevance," actually? Frankly, we do not know. We do not know it any more than we know what is information, or energy, or matter, or gravity, or life, or any number of other basic notions and phenomena. Scientist dealing with these will freely admit the proposition of "*we do not know.*" Instead, of trying to answer the question directly they are busy investigating the nature, manifestations, behavior, and effects of these phenomena and notions. Newton, Galileo, Einstein did exactly that in physics, as did Watson and Crick in molecular biology.

Spurred by striking advances in applications of information technology to handling of information in general and of relevant information in particular, relevance itself became a subject of scientific investigation. *What is the nature of relevance? What are its manifestations? Behavior? Effects?*

There are two reasons for addressing these questions. Both are time honored. One is knowledge for knowledge's sake: to better understand relevance. The other is pragmatic: we assume that the more we know and understand about relevance the better we can build systems, algorithms, and processes aimed at retrieving relevant information.

From its start shortly after the end of the Second World War, one of the main orientations of information science is toward developing and deploying ways and means for retrieval of relevant information by using advances in information technology. Not surprisingly then, investigation of the notion of relevance became a research topic on its own.

Note that the book is in large part based on previous studies of relevance by the author:

Saracevic, T. (1975). Relevance: A Review of and a framework for the thinking on the notion in information science. *Journal of the American Society for Information Science*, 26(6), 321–343.

Saracevic, T. (2007a). Relevance: A review of the literature and a framework for thinking on the notion in information science. Part II: nature and manifestations of relevance. *Journal of the American Society for Information Science and Technology*, 58(3), 1915–1933.

Saracevic, T. (2007b). Relevance: A review of the literature and a framework for thinking on the notion in information science. Part III: Behavior and effects of relevance. *Journal of the American Society for Information Science and Technology*, 58(13), 2126–2144.

Saracevic, T. (2008). Effects of inconsistent relevance judgments on information retrieval test results: A historical perspective. *Library Trends*, 56(4), 763–783.

Saracevic, T. (2016). Relevance: In search of a theoretical foundation. In: Sonnenwald, D. (ed.), *Theory Development in the Information Sciences*. Austin: University of Texas Press.

Tefko Saracevic
July 2016

CHAPTER 1

Introduction

Everybody searches. Everybody googles. In doing so, everybody is looking for something that is relevant to whatever current question, state, problem. And everybody knows what relevance is. It is a "y'know" notion, concept, idea—no need to explain whatsoever. This is true from one end of the globe to another. And this is the basic, underlying reason why search engines and other systems with similar goals are so wildly successful throughout the globe. They need no explanation as to what they are all about. They are about relevance.

Searching for relevant information using information technology became a ubiquitous activity in contemporary information society. *Relevant* information means information that pertains to the matter or problem at hand—it is directly connected with effective communication. A significant economic component is involved in these activities. Searching is not only ubiquitous; it became big business as well. Relevance is involved in all that.

The basic objective of all information retrieval (IR) systems, including contemporary search engines and abstracting and citation systems of all kinds, is to provide relevant information to users in response to their queries or profiles and (hopefully) information needs. Garcia-Molina et al. (2011) refer to them under a generic name "*information providing mechanisms*" and conclude that:

> "... *one of the fundamental problems in computer science has become even more critical today: how to identify objects satisfying a user's information need. The goal is to present to the user only information that is of interest and relevance, at the right place and time.*"
> (ibid., 21)

Queries and profiles could be explicit or implicit; retrieval methods and algorithms could vary widely; displays could differ; coverage could fluctuate in breadth and depth ... but no matter what the operation, still the basic intent is to present users not with any old kind of information, but with relevant information. The basic goal of all research and development (R&D) in IR systems (or information-providing mechanisms) in computer science is improving the relevance of the results to the query. In that sense, relevance is the basic notion underlying any and all IR systems. It underlies Google, Baidu, and all other search engines; Amazon and other systems with recommendations; advertising systems geared toward individuals or identified groups; Web of Science, Scopus, and all indexing and citation databases; and searching the content of complex websites, such as the Library of Congress. Relevance is "the invisible hand" that governs these systems.

The notion of the "invisible hand" is taken from Adam Smith (1723–1790), regarded as the father of economics. In his classic 1776 book *An Inquiry into the Nature and Causes of the Wealth of Nations* Smith set out the mechanism by which he believed economic society operated; among others, he explained market decisions as often being governed by an "invisible hand." In the same spirit, while the hand of relevance is invisible, it is governing.

1.1   INFORMATION TECHNOLOGY AND RELEVANCE

In human history, relevance has been around forever, or as long as humans tried to communicate and use information effectively. Modern computers have been around since the 1950s, the Internet started its rise in the 1970s, the Web in the 1990s, and social media in the 2000s. In this short time, contemporary information technology (IT), which includes modern communication technology, social media, and information systems based on IT, changed and transformed a great many things in society—from education to health care, from earning a living to leisure, from physics to classics, from government to being governed, from being young to being old. IT changed information activities dramatically, namely the way we acquire, organize, store, preserve, search, retrieve, communicate, interact with, and use information. In all of those information activities relevance plays a most significant, underlying, and yet elusive role.

When people use IT for information activities, particularly searching, relevance is the primary underlying reason. As far as people are concerned, relevance is tacitly present and inescapable. Correspondingly, relevance plays a significant, underlying role when these activities are performed by IR systems (or information-providing mechanisms) as

> A note on information objects, i.e., entities potentially conveying information: They can take many forms, such as documents (historically first treated in IR and still in great many cases), but also extended now to facts, music, spoken words, still and moving images, artifacts, and other forms of human expression.

well; because these systems are designed primarily to respond with information or information objects that are potentially relevant to people. In this lies the significance of relevance.

The reason we position people and IT together in the discussion above is to point out some basic premises, distinctions, problems, and conflicts. IR systems use a variety of methods, algorithms, and technologies aimed at organization of information or information objects and subsequently aimed at searching for and retrieval of information (or information objects) that may be potentially relevant to users; for shorthand, we label this "*systems relevance.*" People go about their ways and assess their own version of relevance; we label this "*human relevance.*" Both treat relevance as a relation (as explained more fully in Section 3.3). However, each may have different premises for what is involved in the relation and in assessing that relation. There are two interacting worlds—the systems world and the human world—and two basic categories of relevance—systems' and humans.' The two worlds interact with various degrees of problems and conflict, from none to a lot.

Our concern here is with the human world of relevance. Relevance is treated here as a human condition, which it is. While we can never get far from systems and associated technology, this book does *not* cover how systems deal with relevance. It does *not* deal with algorithms. Treatments of relevance in information retrieval—in algorithms, measures, evaluation—are beyond the scope of this book. There are plenty of books, articles, proceeding papers, lectures, and musings that deal with these topics. However, relevance is at the heart of such systems and algorithms. All are geared toward relevance.

1.2   PURPOSE, OBJECTIVES, ORGANIZATION

Spurred by advances in information retrieval (IR) and information systems of various kinds in handling of relevance, a number of basic questions were raised:

> *But what is relevance to start with? What are some of its properties and manifestations?*
> *How do people treat relevance? What affects relevance assessments?*

Following these basic questions, over the past half a century or so the nature, manifestation, behavior, effects, and problems related to human relevance were investigated in a number of fields, but primarily in information science and to some degree in computer science. Relevance research is multidisciplinary. The purpose here is to trace the evolution and with it the history of thinking and research on relevance in information science and related fields from the human point of view. To repeat: The book does not deal with the technological and algorithmic point of view, namely, it does *not* address how systems deal with relevance as related to information or information objects.

The objectives are to present the results of this thinking and research in a way that may be useful not only for enhancing a general understanding of the notion of relevance but also, hopefully, for attempts to incorporate some of that understanding in design and operations of information retrieval systems, search engines included (more about that in Section 9.3). The history of science and technology is full of instances where a better understanding of the basic notions or phenomena underlying a technology led to development of more effective and successful technologies and systems. A fruitful, though sometimes convoluted and arduous, translation was realized. I hope that a better understanding of relevance may lead to better information systems. This clearly illustrates the significance of relevance research. Considering and understanding relevance as a notion is still relevant, if not even more so, to building and operating information systems—now ever more complex in the Web environment—that effectively provide information to users pertaining to their problems at hand.

This book evolved also in part from a series of relevance lectures: individual chapters can be referred to and used as a series of individual lectures covering various aspects of thinking, research, and experimental findings on relevance.

In addition to the Introduction (Chapter 1), discussing the relation between contemporary developments in information technology and relevance, the book as a whole is further organized in eight chapters covering different topics.

- Chapter 2 provides a *historical overview* with concentration how information retrieval was linked to relevance.

- Chapter 3 focuses on general and specific understandings about *manifestations and attributes of relevance*.

- Chapter 4 reviews various proposed *models of relevance* and describes some of them in detail.

- Chapter 5 is devoted to *theories of relevance* in several fields and examines their application in information science.

- Chapter 6 enumerates experimental studies that provided observation and data on *behavior of relevance* concentrating on determination of what makes information or information objects relevant.

- Chapter 7 enumerates experimental studies that provided observation and data on *effects of relevance* concentrating on relevance judges and judgments and their effects on results of IR tests.

- Chapter 8 enumerates experimental studies that analyzed effects of *inconsistent relevance judgments* on IR test results.

- Finally, Chapter 9 provides some general *conclusions* about relevance research and trends.

Each chapter, including this one, concludes with a synthesis that in effect provides a digest and interpretation of contemporary thinking on the topic treated or suggests hypotheses for future research.

1.3   SYNTHESIS: BASICS ABOUT RELEVANCE

Here are some basic issues and realities about relevance:

◊ Searching for relevant information using technology became a ubiquitous activity in contemporary information society.

◊ As far as people are concerned relevance is a "y'know" notion, concept, idea—no need to explain or define it whatsoever. This is true from one end of the globe to another.

◊ The basic objective of all information retrieval (IR) systems, including contemporary search engines and information retrieval systems of all kinds, is to provide relevant information to users in response to their queries or profiles and, hopefully, needs.

◊ There are two interacting worlds—the systems world and the human world—and two basic categories of relevance—systems' and humans.' The two worlds interact with various degrees of problems and conflict, from none to a lot.

◊ Relevance is "the invisible hand" that governs all kinds of information retrieval systems and information-providing mechanisms.

CHAPTER 2

A Bit of History

"Those who don't know history are doomed to repeat it."
Edmund Burke (1729–1797)

2.1 INFORMATION SCIENCE

Debate and research about relevance have a pragmatic foundation. Historically, contemporary concerns with relevance as a notion stem from operational and down-to-earth problems related to retrieval of relevant information in information science.

Dictionaries and encyclopedias routinely define information science[1] as the science dealing with the effective collection, storage, and retrieval of information. More specifically, information science is a field of professional practice and scientific inquiry addressing the problem of effective communication of knowledge records—no matter the form: print, electronic, image, sound— among humans in the context of the social, organizational, and individual need for and use of information (Saracevic, 1999). The key orientation here is the problem of need for and use of information, as involving knowledge records of all kinds in all media. To provide for that need, information science deals with specifically oriented information techniques, procedures, systems, and technologies. However, for understanding of information science, as of any other field, of interest is not only a lexical definition but also (and even more so) the description of problems addressed. A field is defined by problems addressed.

Information science is a field that emerged in the aftermath of the Second World War, along with a number of new fields, with computer science being but one example. The rapid pace of scientific and technical advances that were accumulating since the start of the 20th century produced by midcentury a scientific and technical revolution. A most visible manifestation of this revolution was the phenomenon of "information explosion," referring to the unabated, exponential growth of scientific and technical publications and information records of all kinds. The term "information explosion" is a metaphor, as is "population explosion," because nothing really exploded but just grew at a high rate, if not even exponentially. The phenomenon of information explosion is continuing and even accelerating to this day, particularly in the digital and Web environments. Addressing the problems of dealing with information explosion is at the heart of information science.

---

[1] https://en.wikipedia.org/wiki/Information_science

The impetus for the development of information science, and even for its very origin and agenda, can be traced to a 1945 article, "As we may think,"[2] by Vannevar Bush (1890–1974),[3] a respected MIT scientist and, even more importantly, the head of the U.S. scientific effort during WWII (Bush, 1945). In this influential article, Bush did two things: (a) he succinctly defined a critical and strategic problem that was on the minds of many, and (b) proposed a solution that was a "technological fix," and thus in tune with the spirit of time. Both had wide appeal and Bush was listened to because of his stature. He defined the problem in almost poetic terms as:

> "*The summation of human experience is being expanded at a prodigious rate, and the means we use for threading through the consequent maze to the momentarily important item is the same as was used in the days of square-rigged ships*" (ibid. Section 1).

In other words, Bush addressed the problem of information explosion. The problem is still with us, even growing.

His solution was to use the emerging computing and other information technology to combat the problem. However, he went even further. He proposed a machine named Memex,[4] incorporating (in his words) a capability for "*association of ideas,*" and duplication of "*mental processes artificially.*" A prescient anticipation of information science and artificial intelligence is evident. Memex was never built, but to this day is an ideal and, some think, a utopia. We are still challenged by the ever-worsening problem of information explosion, now universal and in a variety of digital formats. We are still trying to fix things technologically. We are still aspiring to incorporate Memex's basic ideas in our solutions of finding what Bush called the "*momentarily important item,*" meaning a relevant item.

Figure 2.1: Vannevar Bush (1890–1974). Courtesy MIT Museum.

A number of scientists and professionals in many fields around the globe listened and took up Bush's challenge. Governments and politicians listened as well and provided funding. The reasoning went something like this: Because science and technology are strategically important for society, efforts that help them, information activities in particular, are also important and need

2   http://www.theatlantic.com/magazine/archive/1945/07/as-we-may-think/303881/
3   http://www.livinginternet.com/i/ii_bush.htm
4   https://en.wikipedia.org/wiki/Memex

support. In the U.S., this led to support of research and development in information retrieval and to some extent relevance research as well, mostly through the National Science Foundation (NSF).

Talking about NSF support: NSF led a multi-agency funding under the same mentioned mandate run by Division of Information & Intelligent systems under Michael Lesk entitled Digital Library Initiatives (DLI); DLI 1 ran 1994–1998; DLI 2 1999–2004. In 1994, the first six awards were made. One of them supported a Stanford University project led by Hector Garcia-Molina and Terry Winograd. Within that project Garcia-Molina's students Larry Page and Sergei Brin collaborated on a system named BackRub that became Google. In the original paper about Google, Brin and Page (1998) acknowledged support from NSFs Digital Library Initiative for development of Google (note that there are various versions of this paper, some have the acknowledgment, others don't). NSF has a story "On the Origins of Google"[5] on its site. There is a continuum from Bush to Google.

Bush was also instrumental in establishing the National Science Foundation (NSF) in the U.S.

The National Science Foundation Act of 1950 (P.L. 81–507) provided a number of mandates, among them "to foster the interchange of scientific information among scientists in the U.S. and foreign countries" (Section 3(a)3) and "to further the full dissemination of [scientific and technical] information of scientific value consistent with the national interest" (Section 11(g)). The 1958 National Defense Education Act (P.L 85–864) (the "Sputnik act") enlarged the mandate: "The National Science Foundation shall [among others] undertake program to develop new or improved methods, including mechanized systems, for making scientific information available" (Title IX, Section 901). By those mandates, an NSF division, which after a number of name and direction changes is now called the Division of Information and Intelligent Systems (IIS), has supported research in these areas since the 1950s.

2.2   INFORMATION RETRIEVAL (IR)

Right after the Second World War a variety of projects started applying a variety of technologies to the problem of controlling information explosion, particularly in science and technology. In the beginning, the technologies were punched cards and microfilm, but soon after computers became available the technology shifted to and stayed with computers. Originally, they begun and evolved within information science and specific fields of application, such as chemistry. By the mid-1960s computer science joined the efforts in a big way.

Various names were applied to these efforts, such as "machine literature searching," or "mechanical organization of knowledge" but by the mid-1950s "information retrieval" prevailed.

[5] http://www.nsf.gov/discoveries/disc_summ.jsp?cntn_id=100660&org=IIS

Actually, the term "information retrieval" (IR) was coined by mathematician and physicist Calvin N. Mooers,[6] a computing and IR pioneer, just as the activity started to expand from its beginnings after World War II. He posited that:

> *"Information retrieval is ... the finding or discovery process with respect to stored information ... useful to him [user]. Information retrieval embraces the intellectual aspects of the description of information and its specification for search, and also whatever systems, technique, or machines that are employed to carry out the operation"* (Mooers, 1951, p. 25).

Over the next half century, information retrieval[7] (IR) evolved and expanded widely. In the beginning, IR was static; now it is highly interactive. It dealt only with representations—indexes, abstracts—now it deals with full texts as well. It previously concentrated on print only; now it covers every medium, and so on. Advances are impressive. However, in a basic sense, IR continues to concentrate on the same fundamental things Mooers described. Searching was and still is about retrieval of relevant information or information objects.

It is of interest to note what made IR different from many other techniques applied for control of information records over a long, historical period. The key difference between IR and related methods and systems that long preceded it, such as classifications, subject headings, various indexing methods, or bibliographic descriptions, including the contemporary Functional Requirements for Bibliographic Records (FRBR) (IFLA, 1998), is that IR specifically included "specification for search." The others, including FRBR, did not. In these long standing techniques what user needs are and should be fulfilled were specified (rather briefly), but how the search will be done was neither specified, nor mentioned at all. Data in bibliographic records were then organized in a way to fulfill the specified needs. Searching was assumed and left to itself—it just happens. In IR, the user's needs are assumed as well, but the search process is specified in algorithmic detail, and data is organized to enable the search. Search engines are about searching to start with; everything else is subsumed to that function.

The fundamental notion used in bibliographic description and in all types of classifications or categorizations, including those used in contemporary databases, is aboutness. The fundamental notion used in IR is *relevance*. As mentioned, it is not about any kind of information, and there are a great many, but about *relevant* information. Fundamentally, bibliographic description and classification concentrate on describing and categorizing information objects; IR is also about that but, *and this is a very important "but,"* in addition IR is about searching as well, and searching is about relevance. Very often, the differences between databases and IR were discussed in terms of differences between structured and unstructured data, which is OK, but the fundamental difference

---

[6]   http://www.nsf.gov/discoveries/disc_summ.jsp?cntn_id=100660&org=IIS
[7]   https://en.wikipedia.org/wiki/Information_retrieval

is in the basic notion used: *aboutness* in the former and *relevance* in the latter. Therein similarity and difference lie. *Relevance entered as a basic notion through the specific concentration on searching.*

By choosing relevance as a basic, underlying notion of IR, related information systems, services, and activities—and with it, the whole field of information science—went in a direction that differed from approaches taken in librarianship, documentation, and related information services, and even in expert systems and contemporary databases in computer science.

For example, the basis of expert systems is uncertainty (or rather reduction of uncertainty based on if–then rules). As a result, expert systems are very different from IR systems. In comparison to IR, expert systems are not as widely adapted and used; actually, they disappeared; presently the designation "expert systems" is used rarely or not any more at all. One of the reasons may be due to the choice of the underlying notion. Relevance is a human notion, widely understood in similar ways from one end of the globe to the other. Uncertainty is not. Besides, the assumption that information decreases uncertainty does not hold universally; information may also increase uncertainty.

2.3   TESTING OF IR SYSTEMS AND FIRST CONCERNS WITH RELEVANCE

Historically, relevance actually crept in unannounced. At the start of IR in the 1950s, nobody actually made a big point about it. IR systems were constructed to do relevance, but nobody talked about it. Still, principles posited then are valid to this day. It was, and still is, accepted that the main objective of IR systems is to retrieve information relevant to user queries, and possibly needs, or as Mooers observed in the above definition, "useful to user."

Actually, the first discussions directly involving relevance in the early 1950s were not about relevance, but about non-relevance, that is about "false drops" or noise—unwanted information retrieved by IR systems. The concerns were about getting too much non-relevant information; subsequently efforts were directed toward development of methods for decreasing of false drops. In other words, the concerns over relevance started with the large amount of non-relevance that endangered effective communication. The problem is still with us.

In mid the 1950s Allen Kent (1922–2014) and James W. Perry (1907–1971), both chemists and pioneers in information science, wrote a series of articles about techniques of IR. In one of the articles, they suggested measures for evaluating performance of IR systems. They called them "precision" and "relevance" (later because of confusion renamed "recall") (Kent et al., 1955). This was the first full recognition of relevance as an underlying notion of retrieval—relevance was the criterion for these measures. Precision and recall measure the probability of agreement between what the system retrieved/did not retrieve as relevant (systems relevance) on the one hand and what the user assessed as relevant (user relevance) on the other hand, with user relevance being the base for deriving probabilities of agreement. *User relevance was and still is treated as the gold standard for performance evaluation.* Over time, many other measures were suggested, but did not take. Precision and recall remained standard measures of effectiveness to this day, with some variations on the theme. Relevance became and remained the underlying criterion for measuring the effectiveness of IR. By now, it is cemented there.

Very soon, after IR systems appeared, the perennial questions asked of all systems were raised: *What is the effectiveness and performance of given IR approaches? How do they compare?* It is not surprising that these questions were raised in IR. At the time, most developers, funders, and users associated with IR were engineers, scientists, or worked in related areas where the question of testing was natural, even obligatory.

The first attempt at IR testing was reported by Gull (1956); relevance judgments were critical in collapse of that test (since the aftermath of results affected IR testing to this date, the experiment is described in some detail in the sidebar). Relevance came to the fore. Ever since all who were engaged with IR testing or their critiques became very sensitive about relevance and relevance judgments. In other words, what is used today as to determining relevance in IR tests has its roots in a collapse of a study in the early 1950s. IR testing continued to this day. Precision and recall (with a number of variations) remained standard measures of effectiveness. A lesson from the first test was learned, although today hardly anybody knows its source. All IR tests include a single judge (or sometimes a group with a consensus) that provide a golden rod of relevance of documents (information sources) against which a system or algorithm performance is assessed.

Gull (1956) reported on an attempt to test the performance of two competing IR systems developed by separate groups: one developed by the Armed Services Technical Information Agency (ASTIA) using subject headings, and the other by a company named Documentation Inc., using uniterms (keywords searched in a Boolean manner). Each group searched 98 requests using the same 15,000 documents, indexed separately, in order to evaluate performance based on relevance of retrieved documents. *However, each group judged relevance separately.* Then, not the systems' performance, but their relevance judgments became contentious. The first group found that 2,200 documents were relevant to the 98 requests, while the second found that 1,998 were relevant. There was not much overlap between groups. The first group judged 1,640 documents relevant that the second did not, and the second group judged 980 relevant that the first did not. They tried to reconcile, considering each other's relevant documents, and again comparing judgments. At the end, they still disagreed; their rate of agreement, even after peace talks, was 30.9%. That did it. The first ever IR evaluation did not continue. It collapsed. The lesson was learned: *Never, ever use more than a single judge (or a single object, such as source document) for establishing the gold standard for comparison. No IR test ever does.*

IR testing began in the late 1950s within a certain context as described by Cyril Cleverdon[8] (1914–1997), an IR testing pioneer, in his acceptance speech for the 1991 Gerard Salton Award given by the Special Interest Group on Information Retrieval (SIGIR), Association for Computing Machinery (ACM):

> *"These new techniques [uniterms, coordinate indexing] generated considerable argument, not only between the proponents of the different systems, but also among the library establishment, many of whom saw these new methods as degrading their professional mystiques … Most of this could be ignored, such as the comment,* 'You had no right to be so intelligent with the Uniterm system; it is meant to be used by persons of low intellect.'… *Controversy over the new methods was still raging, with extravagant claims on one side being countered by absurd arguments on the other side, without any firm data being available to justify either viewpoint* (Cleverdon, 1991, pp. 3, 5)."

Testing continued with pioneering and even legendary tests at the Cranfield Institute of Technology in the UK (thus "Cranfield tests"). There were two periods for these tests: Cranfield 1 ran from 1957 to 1961 and Cranfield 2 from 1963 to 1966 (Cleverdon, 1967; 1991). Reports from various Cranfield tests are reproduced in the SIGIR Museum.[9] The most important result from Cranfield tests was the finding that complex, controlled, classificatory indexing schemes were not necessary for effective retrieval; keywords worked as well. This justified pioneering development of algorithm-based IR by Gerard ("Gerry") Salton (1927–1995) and his SMART system with numerous experiments (Salton, 1969).

Among others, Cranfield tests established the traditional model of IR (presented in Figure 4.1) and an associated test methodology still in use today in the majority of IR tests. IR testing culminated with Text Retrieval Conference (TREC)[10] established in 1992 and continuing to this day.

IR tests are about comparing effectiveness of different retrieval methods. (Excellent historical syntheses of various IR tests from the Cranfield tests to TREC are in Robertson (2008) and in a Morgan & Claypool book by Harman, 2011). All these tests used relevance as the basic criterion and user relevance judgments as the gold standard for comparison. However, they also had an important unintended consequence. Relevance assessments used in early tests became contentious; it quickly became clear that relevance itself is a problem. Relevance assessments were revealed, among others, not

> TREC is a long-term, ongoing effort at the (U.S.) National Institute for Standards and Technology (NIST) that brings various IR teams around the world together annually to compare results from different IR approaches under laboratory conditions (Vorhees and Harman, 2005).

---

[8] https://en.wikipedia.org/wiki/Cyril_Cleverdon
[9] http://sigir.org/resources/museum/
[10] http://trec.nist.gov/

to be consistent (surprise! surprise!) which brought calls for better definition of relevance and its properties. A number of efforts were aimed at that direction, as summarized in the next chapter (Section 3.2).

2.4   BEGINNING OF RELEVANCE EXPERIMENTS

Experiments dealing with relevance began at the start of 1960s in part stimulated by a desire to improve IR procedures and in part as a reaction to relevance problems uncovered in IR testing. The first experiments that involved relevance in the realm of information science were reported by Rath et al. (1961) and Resnick (1961) (at the time all worked at the IBM Research Center, Yorktown Heights, NY, where pioneering work on computer applications for IR was done). These first experiments brought along an unintended consequence of their own which continued for decades: they confused the notion of *relevance* with *relevance judgment*. While related, they are still two different things. The first one is a notion, a concept; the second one is an action upon the notion or concept—the difference is similar as between justice and judging, love and loving. Remnants of this confusion show sometimes even today.

The NSF Office of Scientific Information (after a number of name changes presently named Division of Information and Intelligent Systems—IIS) was the major U.S. government funder of projects in the 1950s and 1960s related to information retrieval, indexing, computer related methods, and general information science. Helen Brownson, then director of the Office of Scientific Information, invited Cyril Cleverdon in 1956 to submit a proposal for tests of various IR methods; he did and for the next decade Cranfield tests (described above) were largely supported by NSF. Burt Adkinson, Brownson's successor and director of the same Office 1957–1970, continued support of IR testing; as relevance problems became evident, he initiated a program for support for relevance research.

In the 1960s, out of that program came funding for the two largest relevance research projects to date. The first one was conducted by a group from Systems Development Corporation (SDC) under Carlos Cuadra and Robert Katter as Principal Investigators (PIs), and the second one by a group from Case Western Reserve University (CWRU) under Alan Rees and Douglas Schultz as PIs; interestingly, three out of four PIs were psychologists—Rees was an English literature major. Both projects became classic, not the least because they established firmly experimentation as a way to investigate relevance. The reports from the projects influenced future relevance research and are cited to this day (Cuadra et al. 1967; Cuadra and Katter, 1967; Rees and Schultz, 1967).

At the time IR testing problems led to support of relevance research. However, this was also the first and last time that relevance research was supported by NSF or for that matter by any other U.S. agency. After the 1960s relevance research continued on its own without any major funding. Relevance research became poor and remained so till this day.

From the first relevance experiments that began in 1961 to 1975 some 15 studies reported on experiments that directly involved relevance, as summarized in Saracevic (1975). For whatever reason from 1975 till 1988 there was a hiatus in relevance experimentation—only one experiment was reported in that period. Relevance experimentation has been revived since. From 1988 till 2007 over 60 experiments have been reported in open literature, as summarized in Saracevic (2007b and 2008). And from 2008 till 2015 some 30 experiments were reported in the open literature, many are summarized in this book.

Cuadra and Katter's team conducted 15 experiments to determine the effects of a number of variables on relevance judgments: article styles; degree of specificity contained in information queries; various definitions of relevance; judgmental conditions and time pressures on judgments; different modes of expressions (scales) in recording judgments; attitude taken by judges about intended use of documents; and amount of academic training of judges. Altogether, there were some 230 subjects—library and psychology students, librarians, and conference attendees.

Rees and Schultz's team conducted a very different single experiment related to three stages of a research project in diabetes to determine effects of a number of variables on relevance judgments: different stages of the research project; various documents and document representations; various groups differing in their subject expertise; different relevance definitions; and different modes of expression. Subjects were 184 judges—M.D.s, Ph.D.s, residents, medical students, and medical librarians.

2.5   SYNTHESIS: HISTORICAL DEVELOPMENTS RELATED TO RELEVANCE

Here are some historical milestones:

◊ Information science emerged after the Second World War, addressing the problem of information explosion in science and technology. Bush's 1945 landmark article, that defined the problem of finding scientific and technical information and suggested a technological solution, affected development of the field.

◊ Information retrieval (IR) was the solution to the problem. The main objective of IR systems was understood from the outset to be retrieval of relevant information. Searching based on relevance was explicitly formulated, later in great algorithmic detail, which set IR apart from previous systems aimed at organization of information.

◊ Most importantly, in the U.S. laws establishing and enlarging the National Science Foundation (NSF) in 1950 and 1958 mandated, among others, funding for R&D in application of technology to information problems. This affected support for many projects not only from NSF but also other agencies and industry. This mandate is operational to this date.

◊ The first recognition of relevance came about in the early 1950s because of concerns with "false drops", noise—and desire to reduce retrieval of non-relevant information or information objects. First formal recognition of relevance came in 1955 with a proposal of precision and recall as effectiveness measures for IR. These measures hold, with a variation on the theme, to this day.

◊ Pressure to test claims about various IR systems and techniques produced first tests of IR systems and techniques in 1950s. Cranfield tests were most significant first test—originally supported by NSF they lasted for about a decade starting in 1957. As a significant legacy these tests produced an IR model and testing methodology used by a majority of IR tests to this day.

◊ IR tests were criticized because of the ways and means of producing relevance judgments. This lead to support for relevance research and experimentation. In the U.S., two large projects supported by NSF concluded in 1967; they are cited to this day. NSF and other agencies in the U.S. have not supported relevance research since then.

◊ First relevance experiments started in 1961. To this day, open literature contains reports from about 100 plus studies involving relevance experimentation, i.e., how people deal with relevance. This does not include a very much larger number of studies and tests on how systems deal with determining relevance algorithmically of information and information objects.

◊ To this day searching, including search engines, is oriented toward retrieval of relevant information. From information related to science, technology, and business coverage has spread to include information in all fields and human endeavors.

CHAPTER 3

Understanding, Manifestations, and Attributes

"Any fool can know. The point is to understand."
Albert Einstein (1879–1955)

3.1 INTUITIVE UNDERSTANDING

"*... relation to the matter at hand.*" This is the meaning of relevance defined in Meriam-Webster[11] and all other major dictionaries. Even without any definition, it is the meaning intuitively understood by peoples everywhere. As mentioned in the Introduction, relevance is a "y'know" notion. They apply it effortlessly, without anybody having to define for them what "relevance" is. It is so basic that people use it without thinking about it. They use it nevertheless and use it all the time. And use it globally.

Intuitively, we understand that relevance implicitly or explicitly always involves a relation. There is ALWAYS, repeat **ALWAYS**, a "*to*" associated with relevance. The "*to*" relates to a context, a matter at hand. Nothing can be relevant if there is no "*to*" involved. The "*to*" may be explicit; but it also may be implied, tacit, unstated—it is there nevertheless.

In communicating with each other, in seeking information, in consulting objects potentially conveying information, in reflection, and in a great many other interactive exchanges, people use relevance. They apply it for filtering, assessing, determining usefulness, inferring, ranking, accepting, rejecting, associating, classifying, joy of discovery ... and for other similar roles and processes. In general, they use it for determining a degree of appropriateness or effectiveness to the "matter at hand." In this sense, we also understand that relevance is not always equal—not every bit of information is necessarily equally relevant to a matter at hand. Thus, relevance may also involve a *measure of relatedness*. Some information or information objects may be more or less relevant than others. Relevance has gradations. Relevance is not necessarily binary.

As they go along, people use relevance *dynamically*—it changes as intentions and cognitive horizons change, or as the matter at hand is modified. Certainly, thoughts are given whether something may be relevant, comparisons as to relevance are made, but without any reflection on the nature of relevance.

We also consider relevance as potentially having different *manifestations* (as further elaborated below). People assess relevance as to, let's say, topicality, usefulness, utility to a given situation

---

[11] http://www.merriam-webster.com/dictionary/relevance

or problem at hand, cognitive fit (what we know and how it fits), temporal aspects (e.g., newest), intent in use, and so on. These manifestations provide a base and context for establishing a rela-tion—they may be explicit or implicit, well-formulated or visceral, rational or not entirely so—all on a continuum. They may be followed even without being stated or even thinking about them.

In other words, relevance is a very basic human cognitive and social notion in frequent, if not even constant, use by our minds when interacting within and without in cases when there is a matter at hand. Relevance is a built-in mechanism that came along with cognition. This may also explain the success and wide use of IR systems, search engines included: people intuitively and readily understand what they are all about. What is actually relevant may not be understood uni-versally at all, but what is relevance is.

From intuitive understanding of relevance, we can derive that it has attributes such as: it is based in cognition; it involves interaction, frequently communication; it is dynamic; it deals with appropriateness or effectiveness; and it is expressed in a context, the matter at hand.

3.2   RELEVANCE DEFINITIONS: … BY ANY OTHER NAME …

Relevance may be expressed by different names. Recall that Bush referred to the "*momentarily important item*" (Section 2.1) and Mooers to "*stored information … useful to [user]*" (Section 2.2). They both referred to relevant information or information objects. Other terms have been used for relevance in addition to *important* and *useful*, such as *pertinent, valuable, of utility, applicable, helpful, appropriate, significant, topical, correspondence, fit, bearing, matching* … and so on. While these terms may have differing connotations, the underlying understanding of relevance remains the same for all of them.

Over years, many definitions of relevance have been offered in information science. The main reason was criticisms that it was not clear what is meant by the notion of relevance—so the whole issue of definition became controversial. From these criticisms emerged a naïve belief that a "good definition" of relevance will make it clear and the controversy will be resolved. However, definitions that were offered were nothing but paraphrases; still, they may be considered as hypotheses enu-merating classes of variables involved.

Definitions fell in a general pattern as illustrated in the sidebar (adapted from Cuadra et al., 1967 and Saracevic, 1975 and 2007a).

A	B	C	D	E
measure	correspondence	document	question	user
degree	utility	article	query	judge
dimension	connection	information object	request	information specialist
estimate	fit	information provided	requirement statement	
relation	match	fact	point of view	requester
appraisal	bearing			person

Relevance is the A of a B existing between a C and a D as determined by an E, where slots were filled with fillers as these:

As to definitions, let us paraphrase Shakespeare: "*What's in a name? That which we call a rose by any other name would smell as sweet.*" That which we call relevance by any other name would still be relevance. Gertrud Stein said in a poem: "*Rose is a rose is a rose is a rose.*"[12]

Relevance is relevance is relevance is relevance.

3.3   MANIFESTATIONS OF RELEVANCE

A manifestation is an indication of the existence, reality, presence, or kind of something. Think of energy: Potential energy and kinetic energy are some of its manifestations. For some phenomena or notions, it is not that easy to identify the variety of manifestations and to distinguish among them. Think of manifestations of love, or information, or relevance. Like many other notions or phenomena, relevance has a number of manifestations.

As mentioned above, relevance indicates a relation. *Always.* Efforts to specify manifestations of relevance have concentrated on identifying what given objects are related by a given kind of relevance. Different manifestations are manifested by different objects being related and/or by different properties used for a relation. Sometimes, the efforts also involved naming different manifestations—such as adding a qualifier in the form of [*adjective*] relevance, e.g., "topical relevance," or using a distinct name to denote a distinct manifestation, e.g., "usefulness." Relevance gained adjectives. Relevance gained names.

3.3.1   BASIC DUALITY

In 1959, Brian C. Vickery (1918−2009) was first to recognize that relevance has different manifestations (Vickery, 1959a, 1959b). His approach also precipitated a pattern of discussion about relevance manifestations that continues to this day. In the first paper in the *Proceedings of the International Conference on Scientific Information* (a highly influential conference and publication), Vickery

---

[12] https://en.wikipedia.org/wiki/Rose_is_a_rose_is_a_rose_is_a_rose

states: the "controlling [criterion] in deciding on the optimum level of discrimination, we may call *user relevance*" (italics his; Vickery 1959a, p. 1277). In the second paper in the same proceedings, he discusses what is meant by "relevant to a particular sought subject" (Vickery 1959b, p. 863). Thus, he identified a duality of relevance manifestations—*user relevance and subject relevance*—and he treated each separately.

User relevance on the one hand and *subject or topic relevance* on the other represent the basic relevance manifestations. Each involves different relations. Each can and has been further refined and interpreted. Each can be thought of as a broad class with subclasses. In IR they dance together, sometimes in intricate patterns and with various levels of success. This is the nature of any and all retrievals of information, and it is why we consider relevance as to be an interaction, as discussed below. The interplay between the two manifestations cannot be avoided; however, the effectiveness may differ greatly depending on how the interplay is accomplished. The two should be complementary, but at times, they are in conflict.

To this day, IR testing is based on comparing *user relevance* (a user's or a surrogate's assessment as to the relevance of retrieved answers or of any information or information objects in the system, even if not retrieved) and *systems relevance* (responses to a query that were retrieved and deemed relevant by a system following some algorithm). As mentioned in the preceding chapter, user relevance is the *gold standard* against which system relevance (and with it a system's performance) is measured (Section 2.3). Thus, performance assessment of a given system (or algorithm) is based on, and follows from, human judgments regarding the relevance of information or information objects provided in response to a given query or information need.

During many years after Vickery's pioneering identification of two major relevance manifestations, many additional manifestations were identified—some through observation and others through introspection. Some of the manifestations are referred to by a number of different names, such as pertinent, useful, utility, germane, material, applicable, appropriate, and the like. No matter what, they all connote relevance manifestations, but denote slightly different relations. As already mentioned, relevance will be relevance by any other name.

3.3.2   DIFFERENT MANIFESTATIONS OF RELEVANCE

At the time when disputes about relevance were in full swing, two articles by Stefano Mizzaro caught a lot of attention and were cited many times; both summarized main relevance issues and proposed, among others, a few formalized solutions; and both had catchy titles (Mizzaro 1997 and 1998). The first article, of interest to the preceding chapter, was entitled "Relevance: The whole history." The second article, of interest here, was entitled "How many relevances in information retrieval?" Indeed, how many are there? Mizzaro aimed at a clarification of relevance manifestations by suggesting a classification that accommodates all of them. He proposed that relevance manifestations can be classified in a four-dimensional space: (a) *information resources* (documents, surrogates, information); (b) *representation of user problem* (real information need, perceived information need, request, query); (c) *time* (interaction between other dimensions as changed over time); and (d) *components* (topic, task, context). Those dimensions represent various manifestations of relevance.

Quite a few other works addressed the same issue of relevance manifestations. With time and recognition of a number of problems with relevance, a cottage industry has developed in identifying and naming different kinds or manifestations of relevance, or presenting arguments about various manifestations. Manifestations of relevance also became argumentative.

Here is a summary of manifestations of relevance in information science, mainly following Saracevic (1997, 2007a), Cosijn and Ingwersen (2000), Borlund (2003), Ingwersen and Järvelin (2005), Cosijin (2010), and Belkin (2015):

➢ *System or algorithmic relevance:* relation between a query and information or information objects in the file of a system as retrieved or as failed to be retrieved by a given procedure or algorithm. Each system has ways and means by which given objects are represented, organized, and matched to a query. They encompass an assumption of relevance, in that the intent is to retrieve a set of objects that the system inferred (constructed) as being relevant to a query. Comparative effectiveness in inferring relevance is the criterion for system relevance.

➢ *Topical or subject relevance:* relation between the subject or topic expressed in a query and topic or subject covered by information or information objects (retrieved or in the systems file, or even in existence). It is assumed that both queries and information objects can be identified as being about a topic or subject. Subject aboutness is the criterion by which topicality is inferred.

➢ *Cognitive relevance or pertinence:* relation between the cognitive state of knowledge of a user, and information or information objects (retrieved or in the systems file, or even in existence). Cognitive correspondence, informativeness, novelty, information quality, and the like are criteria by which cognitive relevance is inferred.

➢ *Usefulness or situational relevance:* relation between the situation, task, or problem at hand, and information objects (retrieved or in the systems file, or even in existence). Usefulness in addressing a given task, in decision-making, appropriateness of information in resolution of a problem, reduction of uncertainty, and the like are criteria by which usefulness or situational relevance is inferred. This may be extended to involve general social and cultural factors as well.

> ➢ *Affective relevance:* relation between the intents, goals, emotions, and motivations of a user, and information (retrieved or in the systems file, or even in existence). Satisfaction, success, accomplishment, and the like are criteria for inferring motivational relevance.

Two of these, *topical or subject relevance* and *usefulness or situational relevance*, are treated next at some length, because they have direct implication for IR and for human interaction with IR systems. In addition, these two are the most often discussed and researched manifestations or kinds of relevance.

3.3.3   RELEVANCE AND TOPICALITY

Topical relevance may be inferred from the output of an IR system or completely independent of any system—from any set of information objects, such as from a pile of documents in an office that were gathered there over the years or from a conversation. Topical relevance may not necessarily involve an IR system at all.

Documentary relevance also denotes topical relevance, but is restricted to documents as texts, rather than a whole class of information objects that include not only texts, but other informational artifacts such as images, music, speech, or multimedia. Similarly, *bibliographic relevance* denotes a relation between *metadata* (e.g., descriptions of documents as found in a catalogue) and the *topic or subject under consideration.*

IR systems derive topical relevance algorithmically, based on a relationship between objects in the system and terms in a query, with possibilities of relevance feedback. However, as Huang and Soergel (2013) noted, detecting topical relevance by people is much more sophisticated than content or term matching; instead, it is a process that heavily involves thinking and reasoning, or cognition in general.

Not surprisingly, some basic questions were raised: *Does topical relevance underlie all others? Do all other manifestations of relevance follow from topical relevance and does it have primacy among relevance manifestations?* As we can imagine, there are two schools of thought: yes and no.

For the first school of thought, topicality is basic. Information or an information object is topically relevant if it can help to answer a user's question. For instance, Hjørland (2010) considers the "subject knowledge view" of relevance (equated with topical relevance) as basic, "derived from a pragmatic theory of knowledge … that could be interpreted as a positivist epistemology" (ibid. p. 232). Also: At times, topical relevance of information or information objects is determined by expert consensus or even expert fiat. Sources in textbooks are a prime example. Authority plays a role. However, different types of users give different weights to authority, as found in several experiments summarized in Chapter 4.

For the second school of thought, topicality is not basic—there is relevance beyond topicality. Non-topical relevance can be derived from information objects that are not directly topically related. An "aha!" moment can be reached from information or an information object that has nothing to do with the topic of the question, as for instance demonstrated by Harter (1992); he labeled that as "psychological relevance," but the term did not take.

3.3.4 RELEVANCE AND USEFULNESS

Considerations about usefulness squarely fall in that second school of thought: topical relevance is not primary; it does not underlie all other manifestations.

The concept of usefulness has a long history in relevance discussions and literature. Already over two decades ago Hersh (1994) argued that topical relevance

> " ... *is ineffective for measuring the impact that systems have on users. An alternative is to use a more situational definition of relevance, which takes account of the impact of the system on the user*" (ibid., p. 201).

The present IR systems, search engines included, produce answers to queries submitted to them. They follow the system's view that resulted in the classic or traditional model of relevance presented in the next chapter. An overwhelming majority of present IR systems are based on the classic model. Their practice begins and ends with the query that people submit to the system. They do not include at all the human side of the equation. They do not include the user side of relevance.

In reality, people *interact* with IR systems, with information and with information objects. They interact dynamically with all of them. They do not emphasize the computer, which is a machine, after all, but about what one does with the computer, which is to find and manage information. Belkin (2015) powerfully argued the goal of IR in general and interaction is:

> "*...supporting people in accomplishing the task or goal which led them to engage in information seeking, by supporting appropriate interaction with information objects. ... Emphasis [is] on the person (often called the "user") as the central actor in the IR situation; and, understanding interaction as its central process. This position, ... has been in quite distinct contrast, not to say conflict, with "mainstream" IR research, which, until quite recently, focused almost exclusively on information object representation and retrieval techniques, and on models of IR which included the "user" as merely an input and feedback device, if at all, and which has no room for interaction as a process at all*" (ibid., p.18).

This approach brought to the fore, and with a force, an emphasis on usefulness as the manifestation that should, or indeed must be followed. Again Belkin (2015):

> *"The basic reasons for this are that: usefulness is a more general concept than relevance, which it may, in certain circumstances, encompass; usefulness is directly applicable to the goal of supporting accomplishment of goal/task; and, usefulness can be applied as a criterion to evaluation of search sessions as a whole, and to the different intentions during a search session"* (ibid., p.20).

While the concept of using usefulness as a criterion for evaluation of interactive IR systems is a most useful and even a correct selection, the interpretation that "usefulness is a more general concept than relevance" is not. What is really meant is that usefulness is more appropriate than topical relevance as the criterion for evaluating interactions. It certainly is. Namely, the sole criterion for evaluation of IR systems, as they are instituted now, is *topical relevance*. As shown above, relevance has a number of manifestations; among them are *usefulness or situational relevance and topical or subject relevance*—each has a different relation.

3.3.5   SUBJECTIVE AND OBJECTIVE RELEVANCE

Almost from the beginning of IR and relevance history there was a school of thought that wanted very much to make a distinction between relevance that is objective (in a sense of based on facts rather that thoughts or opinions) and relevance that is subjective (in a sense that it exists only in the mind and not independently of it). This is not surprising, since "objective" and "subjective" have well-known connotations not only in popular use, but also in science and research in general.

Summarizing several philosophical works on relevance, Swanson (1986) wrote an often-cited article explicating the differences between subjective and objective relevance. The title of the article "Subjective versus objective relevance in bibliographic retrieval systems" alludes to a tension between the two. He defined subjective relevance as related to users and objective relevance to IR systems. As to subjective relevance, he states:

> *"... The relevance to a request of any book, journal article, document, or other piece of information ... has often been defined by the response of the requester. That is, whatever the requester says is relevant is taken to be relevant; the requester is the final arbiter, it is argued, because an information-retrieval system exists only to serve its users. Relevance so defined is subjective; it is a mental experience. ... Subjective relevance has also been called 'pertinence,' 'utility,' 'usefulness,' and 'psychological relevance'"* (ibid., pp.390, 391).

Surprisingly, he did not define objective relevance fully, but simply associated it with systems that provide response to a request.

The basis for characterizing each remains the same: subjective relevance is associated with users and objective relevance with systems. However, the algorithms in IR (or any other) system are created by their designers; they also differ from one system to the other; thus, they are subjective as well. In other words, there is no "objective" relevance at all. All relevance is subjective, even when given by a fiat. Still, the search for making a distinction between subjective and objective relevance continues to this day, particularly in epistemology (e.g., Allo, 2014).

3.4   HOW DOES RELEVANCE HAPPEN?

The understanding of relevance in information science evolved over time and it was adapted to specific circumstances encountered; however, it closely followed the intuitive understanding and attributes as enumerated. All elaborations followed it as well.

In information science we consider relevance as a relation between information or information objects on the one hand, and contexts which include cognitive and affective states (topic, problem, task, situation, information need, motivation) on the other hand, based on some property reflecting a desired manifestation of relevance (topicality, utility, cognitive match). In addition, we also measure the intensity of the relation on some scale (degree of relevance, or utility, or pertinence). Thus, in information science relevance is a relation and a measure. It is worth stressing that the context is formulated through a dynamic interaction between a number of external and internal aspects, from a physical situation to cognitive and affective states to motivations and beliefs and back to feedback and resolution. Context is complex.

But: *How does relevance happen?* It is not given beforehand. It is inferred. Here comes a very important, if not even a key distinction in information science:

> Users *derive* relevance of information or information objects provided by systems (IR systems, search engines)—as mentioned, we call this *user relevance*. Systems *create* relevance following some or other algorithm and procedure connecting information objects and queries—we call this *systems relevance*. These are two very different processes, even though both are inferences. Users derive relevance based on a relation between a given context and information or information objects as given. Systems create relevance based on a query as given and algorithmic processes that connect queries and information or information objects in the system. Furthermore, the inference—creation or derivation—follows some intent.[13]

Here are four final points about understanding relevance in information science:

1. The process of inference—creation or derivation—follows some *intent*. In other words, intentionality is involved.

---

[13]   Note that *derive* here is used in a sense to obtain by some process of reasoning, and *create* to produce, construct, generate; *create* is not necessarily associated with creativity.

2. Either derived or created relevance usually involves a process of *selection*. Information or information objects are selected as relevant (or expressed on some continuum of relevance) from a number of available existing, or even competing, information objects or information. The selection is geared toward maximization of results, minimization of effort in using the results, or both.

3. The selection process involves a series of *interactions* of various kinds.

4. Relevant information does not mean that it is also *true*. Relevance and truth are not necessarily connected.

Thus, an understanding of relevance also recognizes that a selection and interaction process is involved following some intentionality. Truth may or may not be entangled.

3.5   SYNTHESIS: ATTRIBUTES OF RELEVANCE

We consider relevance as having a number of dimensions or attributes:

Relevance is a relation. Relevance is a property. Relevance is a measure. Relevance has a context, external and internal. Relevance may change. Relevance has a number of manifestations or kinds. Relevance is not given. Relevance is inferred. Relevance is created or derived. Relevance involves selection. Relevance involves interaction. Relevance follows some intentionality.

These attributes of relevance can be summarized as follows (Saracevic 1996, 2007a; Cosijn and Ingwersen, 2000):

◊ Relation: Relevance arises when expressing a relation along certain properties, frequently in communicative exchanges that involve people as well as information objects.

◊ Intention: The relation in expression of relevance involves intention(s)—objectives, roles, expectations. Motivation is involved.

◊ Context: The intention in expression of relevance always comes from a context and is directed toward that context. Relevance cannot be considered without a context.

◊ Internal context: Relevance involves cognitive and affective states.

◊ External context: Relevance is directed toward a situation, tasks, problem-at-hand. Social and cultural components may be involved as well.

◊ Inference: Relevance involves assessment about a relation, and on that basis is created or derived.

◊ Selection: Inference may also involve a selection from competing sources geared toward maximization of results and/or minimization of effort in dealing with results.

◊ Interaction: Inference is accomplished as a dynamic, interacting process, in which an interpretation of other attributes may change, as context changes.

◊ Measurement: Relevance involves a graduated assessment of the effectiveness or degree of maximization of a given relation, such as assessment of some information sought, for an intention geared toward a context.

◊ Truth: Relevance may or may not be connected with truth.

CHAPTER 4

Models of Relevance

"All is flux, nothing stays still."
Plato (c. 428 B.C.–c. 348 B.C.)

4.1 INTRODUCTION

Models are a simplified version of a given reality; they are representations, even idealizations. Models can also be abstractions forming general ideas from specific examples—presented as a description of an entity, process or state of affairs. Models can be conceptual or physical. Models are used in a great many fields, for a great many purposes. Some are defined in the sidebar.

Models and modeling are indispensable for some fields. For instance, cognitive science rests on the assumption that people have mental models—these are investigated at length; in computer science much of architecture and programming rests on construction and manipulation of models.

System models describe important aspects of a reality, e.g., entities in a system and their functions. However, the same system can be described, viewed, from different points of view that predicate given types of actions and exclude other types. Moreover, each and every model rests on some stated or unstated assumptions; often these assumptions have to be investigated.

In summary, the same thing can be represented by different models that may suggest different actions and rest on different

A *scientific model* is a simplified abstract view of a complex reality. It represents empirical objects, phenomena, and physical processes in a logical way.

An *economic model* is a simplified framework designed to illustrate complex processes. It is a theoretical construct that represents economic processes by a set of variables and a set of logical and/or quantitative relationships between them.

In cognitive science and philosophy of mind, a *mental model* is a representation of something in the mind. It is an internal symbol or representation of external reality. User models of relevance fall in that category.

A *system model* is a conceptual model that describes and represents the elements, structure, behavior, and other views of a system or process. It is widely used in system analysis, systems architecture, and computer science. Systems model of relevance (also discussed below) falls in that category.

assumptions. This holds for models involving relevance as well. Several relevance models emerged—relevance is eminently "modelable."

4.2   SYSTEMS VIEW AND MODEL OF RELEVANCE

To set the stage let us start with a few definitions. A system is a set of elements (sometimes called components) in interaction forming a complex whole. Human-made systems are a set of elements in interaction that perform certain functions for a given purpose.

Information retrieval (IR) systems are a set of elements that interact with users for the purpose of retrieving *relevant information* (or information objects) to a user. Over time, several models of IR systems were proposed; a few concentrated on the "big picture" representing general functions and interactions; many others focused on specific functions, such as indexing representations or search mechanisms. A few "big picture" models are described here. Each emphasizes different functions involved in IR, but all take for granted that relevance is involved in their purpose.

The main functions of information retrieval (IR) systems are: *acquisition* of information objects, their *representation* and *organization*, and provision of a search mechanism in response to a query or profile. In turn, the query (a formulated search) results from a question, which is a representation of a user's *information need* as related to a given *problem-at-hand or situation* encountered by a user. As mentioned, in respect to search results, we distinguish between *systems relevance*, output relevant to a query, and *user relevance*, output relevant to a user's problem at hand. That is, we distinguish between a system assigned probability of relevance and a user (or user surrogate) assignment of relevance. The two may coincide to various degrees.

Figure 4.1 is a graphic depiction of such an IR model commonly called the classic or traditional IR model.

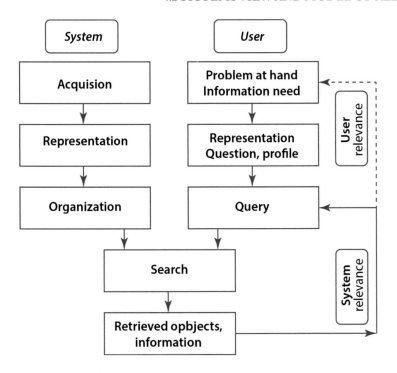

Figure 4.1: Classic model of information retrieval systems.

Historically, the classic IR model emerged informally at the beginning of IR testing in the early 1960s as reflected in the reports of Cranfield experiments (done at Cranfield Institute of Technology, UK) conducted by Cyril Cleverdon from 1958 to 1966 as described in Section 2.3. Based on this model, Cleverdon also developed a general methodology for IR testing that became a prototype for subsequent IR tests. The influential SMART tests conducted by Gerard Salton from 1961 until the time of his death in 1995 followed both the classic model and Cranfield methodology. So did the experiments conducted under the auspices of Text Retrieval Conference (TREC) from 1992 to date (Harman, 2011). TREC is organized around individual tracks, each addressing a specific medium, process, or application in IR, but almost all follow the classic model and Cranfield methodology.

In all of these, relevance played a key role with user (or surrogate user) assessment of relevance being the gold standard for evaluating effectiveness of various system or algorithmic performances. In turn, problems encountered with relevance during these tests inspired a vigorous debate, even controversy, and modeling away from the classic model. To a great degree they affected relevance experimentation as well (presented in Chapters 6, 7, and 8).

With variations on a theme, the basic elements, functions, and purpose of the classic model are included in a number of texts, from the classic one by van Rijsbergen (1979) to a more recent one by Baeza-Yates and Ribiero-Neto (2011), and in many articles about IR over past decades. In other words, the classic IR model formulated in the 1960s is still in use in IR depiction and testing over half a century later. It lives on, particularly in IR algorithms and TREC.

However, implementation of various functions through algorithms, principally as to representation and searching, changed and improved dramatically over time, but relevance remained their goal. The what and how are variables in a never-ending process of change; the why is constant.

4.2.1   CRITIQUES

Every model can and has been critiqued—after all, models are simplifications that open them to questioning. The classic IR model is no exception. Two different types of critiques are synthesized here: the first deals with the nature of the model itself, the second with the application of the model in IR testing.

Static vs. Dynamic

First, a number of critiques suggested that a major deficiency of the classic model is depiction of relevance in IR as *static* while in reality the processes involved with relevance are highly *dynamic* and *interactive*. Interaction is missing and ignored. The first major and widely cited critique was by Schamber et al. (1990). They re-examined thinking about relevance in information science, addressed the role of relevance in human information behavior and in systems evaluation, summarized major ideas and experiments, and came to a forceful conclusion that relevance, and with it IR, should be modeled as being dynamic and situational, rather than static. Numerous articles followed, elaborating on the same critique.

IR interaction became a subject of research, such as reported by Borlund (2003), Ju and Gluck (2011), and many others—a comprehensive review on the topic by Kelly (2009) contains over 300 references. For nine years (1994–2002) TREC hosted an interactive track, but the results were meager. The classic model and methodology under which TREC operated did not fit, including relevance assessments, and no new model and methodology was developed.

Of course, dynamic properties of relevance had been discussed in previous decades and demonstrated in experiments as readily acknowledged by the authors, but it was their insistence on the primacy of the dynamic and situational nature of relevance—all is flux—that struck a chord. The ideas from these articles inspired a new wave of relevance experiments and indirectly a separation discussed below.

As discussed previously (Section 3.3.4), Belkin (2015) strongly argued that interaction is what people actually do when using IR systems. In that sense, Belkin's is the strongest in a long set of critiques of the classic model.

All these critiques, all these accounts of the Achilles' heel of the classic model, raise a larger issue. IR testing as practiced over the last half century from Cranfield to TREC uses the classic model and associated methodology where relevance is treated solely from the system point of view, totally ignoring people's activities and interactions. The model is a gross oversimplification of a reality, as readily admitted. However, simplification is widely and successfully used in science all the time. (To illustrate: Galileo (1564–1642), in a study of falling bodies, suggested that falling bodies would fall with a uniform acceleration, no matter their mass—a hammer and a feather accelerated the same—but he assumed a negligible resistance, a vacuum—a simplification, for vacuum is not something found in the reality of the earth.) In the same vein, numerous advances in algorithms for information representation and searching were achieved using the classic model and all that goes with it. Things advanced, got better, much better on the system side. To some extent they also got better on the user side, but not that much better. Therefore, the classic model delivered on one side but not the other.

System vs. User

Second, a number of very different critiques addressed limits of IR testing as practiced. The classic IR model depicts two branches that get together in the process of searching—one oriented toward system and the other toward user.

The system side concentrates on functions necessary to prepare information objects for searching and the conduct of the search itself—how to handle a query. In detail, the system branch of the classic model consists of a set of assumptions or premises and algorithms for ranking information objects in relation to a user's query, creating the system's relevance.

The user side concentrates on the context—problem that produced an information need that underlies the question, which in turn is translated into a query.

As mentioned, this dual orientation produces two distinct relevances: system relevance and user relevance. On the one hand, system relevance is nowadays determined by algorithms processed by machines; on the other hand, user relevance is a result of human information behavior and situational context-at-hand. System relevance tries to approximate user relevance.

Testing of IR systems as widely practiced in laboratories—Cranfield, SMART, TREC—concentrates exclusively on the system side of the classic model and on system relevance, completely ignoring the user side and user relevance. This became a major point of criticism and even discord. Repeatedly and in many ways it has been pointed out that there is a disconnect between how systems (machines, algorithms) determine what may be relevant and how humans decide what is relevant.

4.3 USER'S VIEW AND MODELS OF RELEVANCE

Over the years, the user's view of relevance has been championed in numerous articles. It produced a few models, two of which are reviewed in this section; it also wrought a battle royal summarized in the next one.

4.3.1 STRATIFIED MODEL OF RELEVANCE

A stratified model of relevance, as depicted in Figure 4.2, was proposed and then elaborated by Saracevic (1997, 2007a). Models that view a complex, intertwined object (process, structure, system, phenomenon, notion) in a stratified way were suggested in a number of fields from linguistics to medicine to meteorology to statistics and more. *Stratified* means that the object modeled is considered in terms of a set of interdependent, interacting layers; it is decomposed and composed back in terms of layers or strata.

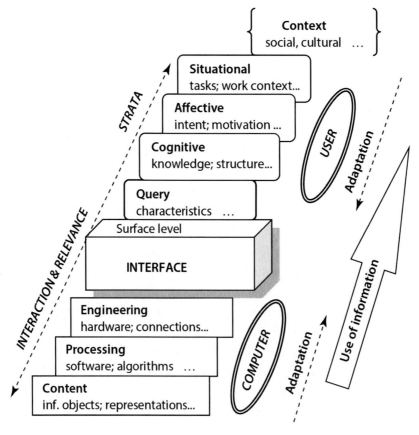

Figure 4.2: Stratified model of relevance interactions. Based on Saracevic, 2007a.

This is an integrative model, meaning that it incorporates a system and user viewpoint. Relevance is placed within a framework of IR interaction. In the stratified model, IR interactions are depicted as involving a number of layers or strata; inferences about relevance are created or derived in interaction and interplay among these strata.

The stratified model starts with assumptions that:

1. users interact with IR systems in order to use information, and

2. that the use of information is connected with cognition and then situational application and context, that is, it is connected with relevance (Saracevic and Kantor, 1988).

The major elements in the stratified model are user and computer, each with a host of variables of their own, having a discourse through an interface. The strata are not necessarily imbedded within each other, nor do they form a hierarchy. The relations and interactions between strata are complex and dynamic.

The user side operates in relation to a context and has a number of levels. Three are suggested to start with: *cognitive, affective,* and *situational.* The suggested computer levels are *engineering* (hardware), *processing* (software, algorithms), and *content* (information resources). It should be recognized that each level can be further delineated or that others may be added, depending on the given set of conditions or emphasis in analysis. Furthermore, situational and/or general context may change, affecting changes or adaptations in various strata; content and other aspects on the computer side may also change, again affecting adaptations. The direction of use follows the second assumption above, namely it is governed by cognitive, affective, situational, and/or broader contextual aspects.

A note on the notion of context: While context has been recognized as a major aspect affecting information seeking in general and relevance in particular, the very notion of what constitutes context in information science is relatively ambiguous, even amorphous—a number of interpretations and models exist, but a consensus of what context entails has not yet emerged (Kelly, 2006). In the stratified model, context is treated as also appearing in strata; from specific situational or work context to more general social (including organizational, institutional, community …) and cultural (historical…) contexts. To a large extent, context(s) determine the problem/situation-at-hand. This corresponds to the notion of "problematic situation" as conceptualized by Schutz and Luckman (1973:116ff). Context is a plural.

When a query is submitted, a variety of interactions are instantiated on the interface or surface level, but the interface is not the focus of interactions despite the fact that it can in its own right effectively support or frustrate other interactions. We can think of interaction as a sequence of processes occurring in several connected levels or strata.

The IR interaction is then a dialogue between the participants—elements associated with the user and with the computer—through an interface, with the main purpose being to affect the cognitive state of the user for effective use of relevant information in connection with an application at hand, including a context. The dialogue can be reiterative, incorporating among other things, various feedback types, and can exhibit a number of patterns—all of which are topics for study.

Each strata/level involves different elements and/or specific processes. On the human side, processes may be physiological, psychological, affective, and cognitive. On the computer side, they may be physical and symbolic. The interface provides for an interaction on the *surface* level in which:

1. Users carry out a dialogue by making utterances (e.g., commands) and receiving responses (computer utterances) through an interface with a computer to not only do searching and matching (as depicted in the traditional IR model), but also to engage in a number of other processes or "things," beyond searching and matching, such as: understanding and eliciting the attributes of a given computer component, or information resource; browsing; navigating within and among information resources, even distributed ones; determining the state of a given process; visualizing displays and results; obtaining and providing various types of feedback; making judgments; and so on.

2. Computers interact with users with given processes and "understandings" of their own, and provide given responses in this dialogue; they also may provide elicitations or requests for responses from the user in turn.

Let me elaborate on the nature of relevance from the stratified model point of view. We assume that the primary (but not the only) intent on both the user and computer side of IR interaction deals with relevance. Given that, we have a number of strata in interaction, and that in each of them may be considerations or inferences as to relevance, then relevance can also be considered in strata. In other words, in IR we have a dynamic, interdependent *system of relevances* (again, note plural). Similarly, this plurality was depicted by Schutz, from whom I took the term "system of relevances," and by Sperber and Wilson, who talked about principles of relevance (elaborated in Section 5.2). In IR, relevance manifests itself in different strata. While often there may be differences in relevance inferences at different strata, these inferences are still interdependent. The whole point of IR evaluation is (or should be) to compare relevance inferences from different levels. We can typify relevance as it manifests itself at different levels and we can then study its behavior and effects within and between strata—as synthesized in Chapters 6 and 7.

4.3.2   INTEGRATED VIEW AND MODEL

A number of works have tried to reconcile the two viewpoints, system's and user's, suggesting integrative relevance models as a resolution to the problem. Starting from a cognitive (thus user) viewpoint, Ingwersen and Järvelin (2005) produced a massive volume outlining the integration of approaches in information seeking and IR in context. The goal of the effort:

*"It is time to look back and to look forward to develop a new integrated view of informa-
tion seeking and retrieval: the field should turn off its separate narrow paths of research
and construct a new avenue"* (ibid., p. vii).

This they did, with relevance playing a major and explicit role. They reviewed any and all
models used in IR and in information seeking research, and produced an extensive model of their
own, integrating cognitive and systems aspects of IR. The Ingewersen-Järvelin integrative model,
anchored in cognition, is complex, reflecting the complexity of the process and situation. The model
has five central components.

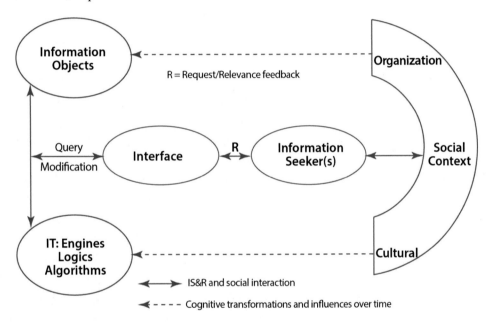

Figure 4.3: Integrated model of information seeking and retrieval (IS&R). Based on Ingwersen and
Järvelin, 2005.

Ingwersen and Järvelin present the model in great detail, modeling and discussing particulars
of each of the components (ibid., Chapter 6, pp. 259–312). Multiple variables, relationships, and
interactions are recognized; their graphic model represented in the figure is really only a framework
for elaboration.

Contexts (plural) play a major role—each of the components has an associated or nested
context. In addition, each component is involved in numerous and varied interactions, depending,
among others, on work tasks, interests, and context. The model is also an integrated relevance
model. In addition, authors defined several manifestations or kinds of relevance as discussed in the
next chapter.

4.4   SPLIT BETWEEN SYSTEM AND USER VIEWPOINTS

Relevance is a participant in a wider battle royal that started way back in the 1980s and is still going on. It involves two opposing views or models of IR: system's and user's. The user's side vehemently criticized the system's side. The systems side barely noticed that it was attacked. A few reconciliatory authors (such as Ingwersen and Järvelin, 2005) tried to resolve the differences—the integrative model and framework presented in the preceding section was the result. In effect the invisible hand of relevance is behind the battle—how to deal with relevance is really what the battle is all about.

As mentioned, the systems viewpoint is based on the classic model of IR, emphasizing the system's processing of information objects and matching them with queries. The user is represented by a query and not considered in any other respect. In other words, the user is taken as a given, thus ignored. Also, interaction is not a consideration.

The user viewpoint considers IR from the user's rather than the system's side, taking the system as a given, thus ignored. The user is considered way beyond the query by seeking to incorporate a host of cognitive and social dimensions, and interaction into the model. The user viewpoint does not have a counterpoint to the widely accepted classic IR model, although a few have been proposed.

Historically, while there were rumblings long before, the frontal attack championing the user side came in a critical review by Dervin and Nilan (1986). While reviewing alternative approaches to the assessment of information needs, they issued a call for a significant paradigm shift in information needs and used research from systems orientation to user orientation, underscoring that the systems approach is inadequate. The review, considered a turning point in user studies, was much cited, often as a sort of a manifesto. The Dervin and Nilan review did not consider relevance per se, but relevance was predominant. Of course, studies of human information behavior (which include information seeking and user studies) can investigate aspects that do not involve relevance. However, when considering any aspect of retrieval and use, relevance is present either explicitly or as an invisible hand.

User studies in a broader context of use of information objects of all kinds have a long history, going back to pre-Second World War. Starting already in the 1960s user studies became strongly oriented toward IR, in the 2000s toward the Web, and in the present decade also on social media. Along the line, they evolved into a broader area of studies of human information behavior. Numerous studies of information behavior emerged, defined by Wilson (2000) as:

> "*The totality of human behavior in relation to sources and channels of information, including both active and passive information seeking, and information use*" (ibid., p. 49).

Relevance became the underlying feature and a key assumption of these studies and models.

Studies of human information behavior burgeoned into an area of its own, with little or no connection with study of IR systems. The former is done under the auspices of information science and many disciplines where use of information is considered, the latter under the auspices of computer science. They became two words looking at different ends of a unified process.

In a massive study of co-citation patterns in information science for the period 1972–1995, White and McCain (1998), among others, mapped the structure of the field, showing two broad clusters or subdisciplines calling them "domain analysis" and "information retrieval":

> *"Specialties can be aggregated upward in two large subdisciplines: (1) The analytical study of learned literatures and their social contexts, comprising citation analysis and citation theory, bibliometrics, and communication in science and R&D; and (2) the study of the human–computer–literature interface, comprising experimental and practical retrieval, general library systems theory, user theory, OPACs, and indexing theory. ...* [Authors] *are essentially "literatures people" or 'retrieval people'"* (ibid., p.337).

Their conclusion: *"Two subdisciplines of information science are not yet well integrated"* (ibid., p. 337) and, *"as things turn out, information science looks rather like Australia: heavily coastal in its development, with a sparsely settled interior"* (ibid., p. 342). White and McCain's conclusion is still valid close to two decades later. This holds for relevance—it indeed has two cultures, each with its own viewpoint and model; they are not integrated, and they map like Australia.

As it turns out, both sides in the battle are wrong. Dervin and Nilan and followers over decades are wrong in insisting on the primacy or exclusivity of the user approach. Systems people are wrong in ignoring the user side and making the traditional IR model an exclusive foundation of their research for decades on end. Neither side got out of their box. Deep down the issue is really not a system versus user approach. It is not system relevance against user relevance. The central issue and problem is: *How can we make the user and system sides work together for the benefit of both?* Belkin (2015) answer is in considering interaction in both research and practice. When IR systems fail, the main reason is a failure in relevance; thus, that is the best reason for advocating the resolution of the system-user problem in an integrative manner.

A number of works have tried to reconcile the two viewpoints, suggesting integrative relevance models as a resolution to the problem. One example of trying to bridge the gap is the work by Ingwersen and Järvelin (2005) described above. In a similar vein, Ruthven (2005) reviews various approaches to relevance, from systems to situational to cognitive, and advocates an approach that integrates IR and information seeking research. While he starts from a systems viewpoint, he also fully recognizes the limited nature of the ensuing relevance definition in that model. Among others, he reviews different kinds of relevance assessments (non-binary, consensus, completeness) and suggests that *"allowing users of IR systems to make differentiated relevance assessments would seem a simple extension to the standard IR interface"* (ibid., p. 71). (Well, is it really "simple"?) He also deals with relevance dynamics—the issue of changing user assessments of relevance over time and comments how IR systems have responded poorly to this phenomenon. Ruthven (2005) rightly concludes:

> *"How we use relevance in the design of IR systems—what evidence of relevance we see as important, how we believe this evidence should be handled, what inference we draw from this evidence—define what we see as the task of retrieval systems"* (ibid., p. 77).

Unfortunately, despite attempts at bridging the two cultures they remain mostly foreign to each other.

4.5   SYNTHESIS: RELEVANCE MODELS

Here are basic subjects and issues addressed in relevance models and modeling over time:

◊ All IR and human information behavior models have relevance at their base either explicitly or as an invisible hand—in effect they are relevance models.

◊ The earliest and most enduring IR model is the classic or traditional model, developed during the Cranfield tests from 1958–1966. A testing methodology was developed along the model. Both became a central feature of a great majority of IR tests to this day. Basically, the same model and methodology have been used in IR tests for some six decades.

◊ The traditional model represents IR in two branches: system's and user's. *Systems relevance* relates output relevant to a query, and *user relevance* relates output relevant to a user's problem at hand.

◊ System relevance is nowadays determined by algorithms processed by machines. User relevance is a result of human information behavior and situational context-at-hand. System relevance tries to approximate user relevance.

◊ Several models were proposed to join together system and user in IR. A stratified model and an integrative model are reviewed here. No model of that type has achieved popularity and widespread application of the classic model.

◊ The classic model has been widely criticized for being static, while the IR process is highly dynamic and interactive and for ignoring the user side.

◊ A split has developed between those studying the system side, concentrating on algorithms, and those studying the user side, concentrating on human information behavior. The former reside mostly in computer science, the latter in information science. They form two worlds, two cultures not communicating well.

◊ A great many human behavior studies involving IR, information use, and relevance claim that the results are "informing system design." This became a mantra. The results are not geared that way. Plus it is very hard to translate human behavior results into specific features in design of systems.

CHAPTER 5

Theories of Relevance

> "There is nothing so practical as a good theory."
> Kurt Lewin (1890–1947)

5.1 INTRODUCTION

A theory is a set of assumptions, assertions, and propositions, organized in a form of explanation or interpretation of the nature, form, or content of a phenomenon, action, or notion. A model (as treated in the preceding chapter) is not a theory. A theory explains, a model represents a reality.

Cleary, the notion of relevance is a great candidate for theorizing. Relevance was extensively treated in information science, but no attempts were made, yet, to formulate an information science-oriented theory of relevance. While the shape of potential theories was debated for a long time (e.g., Park (1994) suggested a possible framework for "a theory of user-based relevance") no theory-cum-theory of relevance emerged in information science. In other words, there is no theory of relevance that came out of information science, not yet.

However, relevance is a universal human notion and thus scholarly work on relevance extended to several fields other than information science. This included formulation of theories on relevance that appeared in logic, philosophy, and communication. Relevance theories in logic were not used in information science (although they were used in IR algorithms), thus are *not* reviewed here. A relevance theory in philosophy was used to some extent in information science, thus a synthesis is provided. Finally, a theory of relevance in communication, formulated in the 1980s and refined in the next decades, had some impact on thinking about relevance in information science, thus it is reviewed here in some detail as theory-on-loan, which is as a theory that is used and interpreted within the context of information science.

5.2 PHILOSOPHY: RELEVANCE IN THE LIFE-WORLD

A number of philosophers, particularly in the area of phenomenology, have been interested in relevance. Of particular interest to information science are two works by Alfred Schutz[14] (1970; and Schutz and Luckman 1973). The latter is a summary of Alfred Schutz's lifelong ideas, posthumously completed by his collaborator, Thomas Luckman.

Briefly, Schutz characterized structure and functioning of the "life-world"—situations that people face in the reality of everyday life. These situations form layers; the life-world is stratified.

---

[14] http://plato.stanford.edu/entries/schutz/

Schutz specified that relevance is the principle for stratification and dynamic interplay among strata. He believed that there is not a single relevance, but rather an interdependent system of relevances (plural). He proposed a typology of relevances with three main categories:

1. *thematic relevances* (in Schutz's 1970 work called "topical"), involving perception of something being problematic;

2. *interpretational relevances*, involving the stock of knowledge at hand in grasping the meaning of that which is perceived; and

3. *motivational relevances*, referring to the course of action to be adopted.

The categories interact. For example, the results of adopted action can motivate the process of obtaining additional interpretative material, and perceptions in thematic relevances may also be affected in this dynamic interaction.

5.2.1   APPLICATIONS IN INFORMATION SCIENCE

These concepts are echoed in many later works on relevance in information science. Schutz is cited a number of times as an appropriate framework for considering relevance in information science. Even when there is not a direct citation to his work, his viewpoint is very much reflected in works on manifestations of relevance. For instance, it is fully accepted in information science that there is not one but several kinds of relevance, i.e., that we are dealing with a "system of relevances" or different manifestations. Categories of relevance elaborated by Schutz are also reflected in different kinds of relevance in information retrieval. All these are discussed in detail in Chapter 3.

Schutz's reference to systems of relevances (plural) suggests a number of manifestations of relevance that are already recognized, and his reference to "horizon" suggests the inclusion of contexts as inevitable.

5.3   COMMUNICATION: RELEVANCE AND COGNITION

Information and communication are related, but there is also a distinction. Information is a *phenomenon*. Communication is a *process*—a process in which information is dispersed or exchanged. The process of communication encompasses a vast array of human activities and has many facets and manifestations. Similarly, the phenomenon of information encompasses many manifestations—there are many kinds of information—and the manifestations are interpreted in many senses. The concept of "communication" can be understood and used in numerous ways (as can the concept of "information"). Not surprisingly, then, the field of communication is broad and expansive. The study of communication intersects with a number of additional fields, including linguistics, semantics, psychology, cognition, philosophy, and related areas; and the study of relevance in communication also comes from an interdisciplinary tradition. Since one of the theories about relevance that emerged in the study of communication was prominently treated in information science, it is described here in some detail.

The most comprehensive and ambitious contribution to theorizing on relevance in a communication framework was made by Sperber and Wilson (1986, 1995) with the latest synthesis published by Wilson and Sperber (2004). Their *Relevance Theory* has the overarching goal of explaining what must be relevant and why to an individual with a single cognitive intention of a conceptual nature. It is based on an inferential model of communication that views communication in terms of intentions, as opposed to the more traditional and widely accepted source-message-destination model (also called the "classical code model," since messages are coded and decoded). The inferential model considers that the critical feature of most human communication—verbal or nonverbal—is the expression and recognition of intentions.

Relevance Theory was originally associated with everyday speech or verbal communication, but later was extended to cover wider cognitive processes. The authors consider it a cognitive psychological theory. It has the ambitious goal of being a theory of both cognition and of communication, tying them together on the basis of relevance. However, the basic problem addressed in the theory is how relevance is created in dialogs between persons.

Relevance explains "*what makes an input worth picking up from the mass of competing stimuli*" (Wilson and Sperber 2004, p. 252). In somewhat awkward language, Wilson and Sperber argue about ostensive behavior (or ostention), manifestations, and presumptions of relevance. Simply put, out of many stimuli, we pay attention only to information that seems relevant to us. Furthermore, to communicate is to claim someone's attention, and hence to imply that the information communicated is relevant. The authors firmly anchor relevance in a given context and talk about contextual effects—relevance is contextual. They also consider relevance assessment as comparative, not quantitative—that is, relevance is comparative.

At the center of their theory, they postulate two principles that they claim reflect universal tendencies:

1. *Cognitive Principle of Relevance*—the claim that human cognition tends to be geared to maximization of relevance, that is, strives to maximize the relevance of inputs; and

2. *Communicative Principle of Relevance*—the claim that every ostensive stimulus conveys a presumption of its own relevance.

In other words, human cognition is relevance oriented, and so is human communication. These two principles lead to the specification of how relevance (of an input to an individual) may be assessed in terms of two components: *cognitive effects* and *processing effort*. That is,

• Other things being equal, the greater the positive cognitive effects achieved by processing an input, the greater the relevance of input to the individual at that time.

- Other things being equal, the greater the processing effort expended, the lower the relevance of the input to the individual at that time (Wilson and Sperber 2004, pp. 252–253).

They explain: "*Humans do have an automatic tendency to maximize relevance, not because we have a choice in the matter—we rarely do—but because of the way our cognitive systems have evolved*" (Wilson and Sperber 2004, p. 254). Treating relevance as an underlying principle in both cognition and communication evokes the Schutz's (1970) explanation of what makes the life-world tick, as mentioned above; however, the life-world was not considered in Wilson and Sperber's *Relevance Theory*.

The two *Principles of Relevance* and the two components of assessment are at the heart of *Relevance Theory*, with the former being explanatory and the latter predictive. Thus, the strength of the theory lies in proposing a number of explanations and operational, predictive principles about cognition and communication in terms of relevance. A relevance theory at last!

Two weaknesses are mentioned here. The first weakness concerns the nature of their proofs and grounds for generalization. They use hypothetical conversations between two protagonists, Peter and Mary, to provide both examples and proof. However, proof by example is no proof. The second weakness is that in three decades since its first appearance, the theory has not been tested empirically or experimentally. A theory is scientific if it is refutable, that is, testable. While the authors proposed a number of possible tests and talked about possible experiments (Wilson and Sperber 2004, p. 283), such tests and experiments have not come forth yet. *Relevance Theory* is appealing, but it is also untested. It awaits verification and possible modification as a result. Of course, the fact that a theory is not tested is not grounds for rejection. However, an untested theory may also be un-testable. In that case, it is not a scientific theory. The question is still open whether *Relevance Theory* is testable. Nevertheless, it does provide a number of insights about relevance and its behavior.

5.3.1   APPLICATIONS IN INFORMATION SCIENCE

Sperber and Wilson's *Relevance Theory* served as a theory-on-loan in two noticeable works, first by Harter (1992) and then 15 years later by White (2007a, 2007b). Both applied *Relevance Theory* to information science in general and information retrieval in particular, but in very different ways.

Harter provided the first attempt to apply *Relevance Theory* to information science in general and to IR in particular. He starts with an emphatic rejection of topical relevance, that is, the notion and practice in IR where relevance is treated as topicality. As a solution, he embraces the notion of relevance as being exclusively related to cognitive states that change dynamically, calling this "psychological relevance." Relevance is what causes cognitive changes in a given context. The essence of

Harter's proposal is to consider a given type, or manifestation of relevance, as the primary or even exclusive aspect of relevance.

Harter deduces a number of excellent insights into relevance behavior. The strength of Harter's notion of psychological relevance is that he attempts to base the concept on a more elaborate theoretical basis, namely *Relevance Theory*. The weakness is that actually he does not do that, beyond borrowing some concepts and terminology. Besides, as with *Relevance Theory*, Harter's construct has not been tested. He discusses, however, the difficulty of testing and applying it in practice. Unfortunately, he did not get there, but he pointed the way and opened a wide-ranging and lively discussion. Still, the value of his attempt to gain some theoretical footing for relevance in information science is in itself groundbreaking.

A second and much more comprehensive attempt to transfer Sperber and Wilson's *Relevance Theory* into an information science framework was made by White (2007a, 2007b). In this massive work, White confines *Relevance Theory* to the application of the *cognitive effects* and *processing effort*, but he does not use their two principles of relevance. In an effort to integrate *Relevance Theory* with IR and bibliometrics, he proposes that cognitive effects and processing effort are also components in relevance assessments in IR and can be used as predictive mechanisms for the operational assessment of relevance. Briefly, White: (a) translates the widely applied IR algorithm based on terms, called tf*idf (term frequencies, inverse document frequencies), into a bibliometric retrieval algorithm based on citations; (b) uses this to create a new two-dimensional visual display of retrieved bibliometric results, called a "pennant diagram" (because it looks like a pennant); (c) interprets the dimensions of the diagram in terms of cognitive effects and processing effort; (d) derives a number of practical examples; and, (e) engages in extensive interpretation of results and discussion of reasoning behind them, in a similar vein as to that of Sperber and Wilson. White has significantly extended their interpretation of *Relevance Theory* to information science circumstances and interests, with both the strengths and weaknesses of the theory present.

The strength of White's interpretation is that he actually applied his constructs to practical work. While the proposed bibliometric retrieval and associated pennant diagram might have been done without recourse to *Relevance Theory*, the borrowed constructs (cognitive effects and processing effort) provided the grounds for extensive abstract explanations of both processes and results. They offer insights about retrieval beyond the statistical nature of the process and rank-listing of results. However, the weakness of the nature of proof present in Sperber and Wilson's work is also present here. Furthermore, White's work is not a test of *Relevance Theory* as claimed; it is structures, concepts, and terminology on loan.

Both works—Harter's and White's—are worthwhile in their efforts to adapt a theory. The field should be stimulated to think about such adaptations and think about theory, but the question remains whether the theory being adapted is worthwhile to start with.

5.4   STILL IN SEARCH OF A THEORY

Authors discussing relevance in information science have not developed any indigenous theory-cum-theory about the notion, nor have they successfully adapted theories from other fields, despite a few attempts. Where theories were borrowed for use, they were merely described, interpreted, and declared appropriate. They were not tested. However, and to their credit, they were conceptual and terminological borrowings used for extending our collective insight about relevance. They made us think.

We are still in search of a theory of relevance applicable to the context of information science, and particularly IR. In other words, we are still in search of a conceptual basis, a set of testable principles and propositions, to explain the notion of relevance applicable to information science practice, to explain its manifestation, and to predict its behavior and effects. An example is an encyclopedic article by White (2010) appropriately entitled "Relevance in Theory."

Of course, practice can be successfully pursued in the absence of a theory. As mentioned, the history of technology has a great many examples of this; IR being just one of them. However, a great many substantial advances have been achieved based on a theory, the history of modern technology has even more such examples.

The attempts to borrow and adapt theories have a positive effect on clarifying empirical knowledge and understanding about relevance in information science. Schutz's reference to systems of relevances (plural) suggests a number of manifestations of relevance that are already recognized, and his reference to "horizon" suggests the inclusion of contexts as inevitable. Sperber and Wilson's cognitive effects and processing efforts suggest dimensions used in assessing relevance, including its dynamic nature, are also well recognized.

5.4.1   WHAT SHOULD A RELEVANCE THEORY ENCOMPASS?

At minimum, a relevance theory in information science should encompass different manifestations of relevance (as enumerated in Section 3.3.2). There, manifestations encompassed: *System or algorithmic relevance*; *Topical or subject relevance*; *Cognitive relevance or pertinence*; *Situational relevance or usefulness*; and *Affective relevance*.

Finally, there are some questions that should be asked in both experiments and theory. As the concept of relevance went global and became widely used, a number of questions emerged. Actually, a great many fascinating questions worthy of research could be asked. Here are but a few (further elaborated in Section 9.2):

- To what extent are the results of relevance scholarship—primarily concerned with a restricted and relatively well-defined population (such as academics, researchers, professionals, students)—applicable to the broad public and every conceivable type of information?

○ Are relevance clues and practices similar or different across the broad public?

○ Is relevance behavior similar or different across the broad public?

○ Can the broad public be defined at all with respect to relevance effects?

It seems that the globalization of relevance also has exposed a need for additional and different agendas for—and approaches to—relevance scholarship.

5.5   SYNTHESIS: THEORY AND RELEVANCE

Here are some basic issues related to theories (or rather lack of theories) about relevance:

◊ Despite a number of efforts, there are no theories related to relevance in information science yet. In that respect IR practice is theory-free.

◊ Theories on-loan about relevance from philosophy and communication were suggested and debated in literature, but did not penetrate either experimentation or practice.

◊ We are still in search of a theory of relevance applicable to the context of information science and particularly IR. In other words, we are still in search of a conceptual basis, a set of testable principles and propositions, to explain the notion of relevance applicable to information science practice, to explain its manifestation, and to predict its behavior and effects. Of course, practice can be successfully pursued in absence of a theory. The history of technology has a great many examples, IR being just one of them. But a great many substantial advances have been achieved based on a theory; the history of modern technology has even more such examples.

◊ A search for an appropriate relevance theory should branch out of philosophy and communication, as currently in vogue. A possible candidate for exploration is decision theory, concerned with issues, such as values and uncertainties, related to given decisions; it is applied in a number of fields.

CHAPTER 6

Experimental Studies on Behavior of Relevance

> "When it is obvious that the goals cannot be reached,
> don't adjust the goals, adjust the action steps."
> Confucius (551 B.C.–479 B.C.)

6.1 INTRODUCTION

Strictly speaking, relevance does not behave. People behave. A number of studies examined a variety of factors that play a role in how humans determine relevance of information or information objects. Relevance behavior studies are related to the broad area of human information behavior, as summarized in an excellent book designed specifically for students and practitioners by Ford (2015). Studies on various aspects of human information behavior, even though related to relevance behavior, are not included here because they are not (pardon me) directly relevant.

White and Wang (1997) studied practices and decisions related to citing of documents—what to cite and what not to cite. Similarly, Kelly (2005) reviewed a host of studies about human decisions during interaction with the Web (or other information resources); the focus was on decisions as to what to examine, retain (save, print), reference, annotate, and the like. Such decisions are assumed to indicate relevance implicitly. In other words, although relevance was not explicitly talked about at all, an action such as citing a document or saving a page is regarded as implying relevance; that is, relevance is not stated, but implied. Although related to relevance by assumption, studies on implicit or secondary relevance are also *not* included here.

In this and the next two chapters, I concentrate exclusively on observational, empirical, or experimental studies, that is, on works that contain data directly addressing relevance. Data is the king.

Studies are briefly summarized following this pattern:

[*author*] used [*subjects*] to do [*tasks*] in order to study [*object of research*].

If the authors had several objects of research, only those related to relevance are mentioned, thus the full statement should actually be read as: "in order to study, among others, [*object of research*]." I do not include description of "among others."

The studies summarized cover a representative sample in the period from about 1990 until the present. The studies are grouped into three areas according to their primary object of study: (1) criteria and clues, (2) relevance dynamics, and (3) relevance feedback.

Principal results from all of the studies, with a number of caveats, are synthesized and generalized at the end of the chapter.

6.2   RELEVANCE CRITERIA AND CLUES

What makes information or information objects relevant to people? More specifically: what do people look for in information or information objects to infer relevance—to decide whether it is relevant or not (or somewhere in between)?

The approach used in studies treated in this section follows the research agenda proposed by Schamber et al. (1990) to study criteria or clues found in given information or information objects (usually documents) that people use in assessments of relevance. Specifically, clues research aims to uncover and classify attributes or criteria that users concentrate on while making relevance inferences. The focus is on criteria users employ while contemplating what is or is not relevant, and to what degree it may be relevant. A wide range of clues or criteria were investigated. Different observational studies came up with differing, and even different, lists and classifications. Of all questions asked in all relevance experiments, the question of clues was investigated the most.

Here are summaries of various studies using a variety of sources:

➢ Schamber (1991) interviewed 30 users of weather information using different sources, from oral reports to documents and maps to derive and categorize their relevance criteria. She identified 22 categories in 10 groups.

➢ Park (1993) interviewed four faculty and six graduate students who received an online search related to their real need to study the thought processes of users evaluating retrieved bibliographic citations. She identified three major categories that included 22 subcategories of variables affecting relevance inferences.

➢ Cool et al. (1993) report on two studies. In the first, they asked approximately 300 freshmen in a computer science course, who were assigned to write an essay on a topic and had selected at least five sources on the topic, to indicate reasons for their selections. In the second study, they interviewed an unspecified number of humanities scholars on their use of information sources for a variety of tasks from teaching to research. Both studies were done to identify characteristics of texts affecting relevance judgments. They identified six facets of judgment of document usefulness.

➢   Barry (1994) interviewed 18 academic users (not specified as being students or faculty) who had requested an information search for documents related to their work to categorize their relevance criteria. She identified 23 categories in seven groups.

➢   Howard (1994) studied nine graduate students who had selected five to seven documents for a class assignment, and identified the relevance criteria for their selections to determine and compare personal constructs (criteria) used in relevance assessments. She identified 32 personal constructs grouped in two groups—topicality and informativeness.

➢   Wang (1997) compared 11 relevance criteria derived from a study in her doctoral dissertation with criteria from four other studies (Schamber, 1991; Cool et al., 1993; Park, 1993; and Barry, 1994) to suggest a general model for document selection using relevance clues.

➢   Fidel and Crandall (1997) studied 15 engineering information users and observed 34 sessions in which they received technical reports, asking them to think aloud about their decisions of deleting or retaining given reports to derive criteria for judging the reports relevant or not relevant. They identified 13 criteria explaining why a report was relevant and 14 criteria explaining why it was not relevant.

➢   Barry and Schamber (1998) compared results from two of their studies (Barry, 1994; Schamber, 1991) to study similarities and differences in derived criteria. They identified 10 criteria in common and concluded that there is a high degree of overlap in criteria from both studies despite the difference in users and sources. This is the only study that attempted a badly needed generalization about relevance clues and criteria with a detailed analysis of data. Other studies that addressed the issue compared different criteria with a checklist or in a brief discussion.

➢   Barry (1998) looked at 18 students and faculty (not differentiated as to how many in each category) who submitted a request for an online search and were presented with 15 retrieved documents. The documents were organized in four document representations to identify the extent to which various document representations contain clues that allow users to determine the presence, or absence, of traits, and/or qualities that determine the relevance of the document. The content analysis identified three broad categories of responses, subdivided into 21 categories of relevance criteria mentioned by these respondents.

➢   Tombros and Sanderson (1998) asked two groups of 10 graduate students each to judge the relevance of a list of the 50 highest ranked documents from 50 TREC queries to investigate the impact of different document clues on the effectiveness of judgments. Each subject judged relevance for five queries; one group judged documents with, and the other without, summaries; judgment time was limited to five minutes. The results indicate that the use of query biased summaries significantly improves both the accuracy and speed of user relevance judgments.

➢   Schamber and Bateman (1999) used a total of 304 graduate students in five studies over several (unspecified) years to sort and rank a number of relevance criteria they used while seeking information, starting with 119 relevance criteria concepts/ terms from previous studies, to interpret and rank user-determined relevance criteria while making relevance inferences.

➢   Hirsh (1999) interviewed 10 fifth-grade children, who searched various electronic sources for a class assignment, about their ways of searching and making decisions. The interviews were done during the first and third week of the project to examine how children make relevance decisions on information related to a school assignment. She identified nine categories of relevance criteria for textual materials and five categories for graphical materials.

➢   Fitzgerald and Galloway (2001) observed 10 undergraduate students using a digital library for their projects in assessing 138 retrieved documents to derive relevance- and evaluation-related reasoning. They identified 11 relevance and 11 evaluation categories of reasoning, both entering in relevance decisions.

➢   Maglaughlin and Sonnenwald (2002) asked 12 graduate students with real information needs to judge the relevance of the 20 most recent documents retrieved in response to the student's own query, which were presented in different representations to derive and compare criteria for relevant, partially relevant, and non-relevant judgments. They identified 29 criteria in 6 categories and compared the presence of their criteria with criteria from 10 other studies.

➢   Choi and Rasmussen (2002) interviewed 38 faculty and graduate students of American History (not differentiated as to faculty and students) on the retrieval of images using the Library of Congress American Memory photo archive to study the users' relevance criteria and dynamic changes in relevance criteria as expressed before and after the search. They used nine criteria before and identified an additional eight criteria after the search.

➢   Toms, et al. (2005) recruited 48 subjects from the general public to search the Web for answers to 16 tasks (topics) in 4 domains. The subjects were asked to indicate in a verbal protocol their assessment of and satisfaction with the results to identify and categorize a set of measures (criteria) for relevance along 5 relevance manifestations as formulated by Saracevic (1996). They identified 11 measures of relevance.

➢   Taylor (2012) in a longitudinal study over several weeks, analyzed responses from some 80 university undergraduate students, 19 to 22 years of age, that had chosen a research topic from a list that was related to course content, in order to evaluate the search behavior of a millennial generation (born between 1982 and 2000) of students conducting information searches in a naturalistic environment searching the Web. Ten criteria for relevance were indentified, of which amount of information ranked highest, followed by recency and depth.

➢   Bilal (2012) analyzed relevance judgments to 30 queries by an unnamed number of kids using search engines: Google, Yahoo!, Bing, Yahoo! Kids, and Ask Kids in order for kids to find information for given tasks reflected in queries and determine precision of relevant and partially relevant hits. Relevance judgments were made by two jurors, not further described. Bilal found that Yahoo! and Bing produced a similar percentage hit overlap with Google (nearly 30%). Ask Kids retrieved 11% in hit overlap with Google versus 3% by Yahoo! Kids. Google performed best on natural language queries; Bing did the same on two-word queries. Precision ratio of relevant hits that Google, Yahoo!, and Bing produced across the queries was below 58%.

➢   Taylor (2013) studied 82 undergraduate students assigned a set of research assignments (work tasks) in order to examine their criteria used to judge relevance of documents found on the Web as related to assignments. They found 758 documents over the 5-week duration of the study and indicated the criteria used to make their relevance judgment by selecting from a predetermined list of 18 relevance criteria. Findings indicate a strong statistical association between work task and criteria used to judge relevance. The criteria of "structure" and "recency" were selected with highest percentages.

➢   Sedghi et al. (2013) used 29 healthcare professionals in a study in order to investigate how healthcare professionals search for and select the medical images they need within medical settings. (Different forms of images, X-rays, and ultrasound/MRI/CRT scans are widely used by healthcare professionals). Using a think-aloud technique and face-to-face interviews, participants were asked to explain how they looked for medical images and how they judged the relevancy of retrieved images. Findings: A total of 15 criteria were applied by participants when determining the relevance of medical images in relation to their information needs. Topicality, followed by image quality and size (dimensions) were the primary and most important relevance criteria used by participants.

➤ Watson (2014) analyzed responses of 37 high-school students undertaking information search tasks, using various data sources (journals, interviews, think-aloud reports, video screen captures, and questionnaires) in order to study criteria and processes that are used by students in their judgments of the relevance of information. Google and Wikipedia were searched most often. Students used titles, summaries (snippets), and connectedness to topic as prime indicators of relevance.

6.3   RELEVANCE DYNAMICS

Do relevance inferences and criteria change over time for the same user and task, and if so, how?

The basic approach used to answer this question starts with two assumptions: (1) as a user progresses through various stages of a task, the user's cognitive state changes and (2) the task changes as well. Thus, something about relevance is also changing. The idea of studying such dynamic changes in relevance has a long history. Rees and Schultz (1967) pioneered this line of inquiry by studying changes in relevance assessments over three stages of a given research project in diabetes. Since then, studies of relevance dynamics follow the same ideas and assumptions. Here is a representative sample of studies on this topic:

➤ Smithson (1994), in a case study approach, studied 22 graduate students with a semester-long assignment to produce a report on a given management information systems topic. Searches for information on the topic were performed by an unspecified number of intermediaries using online databases. To observe differences in judgments at different stages (initial, final, citing) and among different cases, Smithson had the users judge a combined total of 1,406 documents for relevance at the initiation and completion stages of the case. He found that 82% of the documents relevant in the initial stage were relevant in the final stage; 12% of the initially relevant documents were cited, but there was a large individual difference among cases.

➤ Wang and White (1995) interviewed 25 faculty and graduate students (not distinguished as to number) about relevance decisions they made concerning documents in the course of their research to identify relevance criteria used in early and later stages of the subjects' research. They identified 11 criteria in the early stages and another 8 in the later stages of research.

➤   Bateman (1998) studied 35 graduate students during six different information seeking stages in respect to a research paper for their class. The students were asked to rate the importance of 40 relevance criteria in different stages to determine whether the criteria change at different stages. She found the criteria were fairly stable across stages.

➤   Vakkari and Hakala (2000) and Vakkari (2001) studied 11 students over a term taking a course on preparing a research proposal for a master's thesis. They observed the students' search results and relevance judgments at the beginning, middle, and final phases of their work to study changes in their relevance assessment. The share of relevant references declined from 23% in the initial phase to 11% in the middle and 13% in the final phase. They identified 26 criteria in six groups. They found that the distribution of criteria changed only slightly across phases.

➤   Tang and Solomon (2001) report on 2 studies: In the first, 90 undergraduate students who were given an assignment and 20 documents first as a bibliographic citation (called *Stage 1*) and then full text (*Stage 2*) were asked to evaluate their relevance for the assignment; in the second study, 9 graduate students who searched for documents to support their own research also were evaluated at Stages 1 and 2 to identify patterns in change in their use of criteria in the two studies and at different stages (i.e., from representations to full text). They found that there were dynamic changes in users' mental model (criteria) of what constitutes a relevant document across stages.

➤   Anderson (2005) observed two academics involved in scholarly research over a period of 2 years to explore relevance assessments as part of the decision-making process of individuals doing research over time. She identified 20 categories in 10 groups that users focused on in making relevance judgments. Three of the groups relate to determining the appropriateness of information and seven of the groups relate to shaping boundaries to a topic.

6.4   RELEVANCE FEEDBACK

What factors affect the process of relevance feedback?

A short explanation of relevance feedback from the human perspective: I find a relevant document, go through it and, on the basis of something in that document, go on and reformulate my search or identify something else that I should consult.

In information retrieval (IR), relevance feedback (RF) is a technique aiming at improving the query being searched using terms from documents that have been assessed as relevant by users (manual RF), or by some algorithm, such as using terms from top-ranked retrieved documents (automatic RF). Manual RF has a long history in search practices by professionals and users, while automatic RF has also a long history in IR in evaluating RF algorithms and practices. Of interest here is the behavior of people when involved in RF and *not* the means and ways of RF in IR, be it either manual or automatic.

> Koenemann and Belkin (1996) used 64 undergraduate students to search two topics from TREC 2 on a subset of the TREC collection using a non-feedback IR system as a base and three systems that incorporated various types of feedback to assess the effectiveness of relevance feedback. They found that relevance feedback improves performance by at least 10% and is preferred by users.

> Spink and Saracevic (1997) used search logs and interaction transcripts from a study that involved 40 mediated searches done by 4 professional intermediaries on DIALOG databases in response to real information needs to analyze the nature of feedback involving users, intermediaries, searches, and results. The users judged 6,225 retrieved documents as to relevance. The researchers identified 885 feedback loops grouped in 5 categories depicting different types of feedback.

> Jansen et al. (2000) analyzed logs of 51,423 queries posed by 18,113 users on the Excite search engine to determine a number of query characteristics, including the incidence of relevance feedback. They found that 5% of queries used RF.

> Quiroga and Mostafa (2002) studied 18 graduate students who searched a collection of 6,000 records in consumer health on a system with various feedback capabilities. The researchers provided a verbal protocol of proceedings to categorize factors that influence relevance feedback assessments. They identified 15 factors in 4 categories related to users and 3 categories of factors related to documents.

> Ruthven et al. (2003) used 15 undergraduate and 15 graduate students to search 6 simulated search topics on an experimental and a control system in 5 experiments in which they assessed retrieved documents as to relevance to examine the searchers' overall search behavior for possibilities of incorporating manual RF into automatic RF. They found, among other things, that users are more satisfied when RF was available, and that their search was more effective. This is really an IR systems study, as is Koenemann and Belkin (1996), but they are included here to show the human side investigated.

6.5   SYNTHESIS: RELEVANCE BEHAVIOR

Caveats abound. Numerous aspects of the studies reviewed can be questioned and criticized. Criteria, language, measures, and methods used in these studies were not standardized and they varied widely. In that sense, although no study was an island, each study was done more or less on its own. Thus, the results are only cautiously comparable. Still, it is really refreshing to see conclusions made based on data, rather than on the basis of examples, anecdotes, authorities, or contemplation. Generalizations below are derived from the studies reviewed by first examining and then synthesizing the actual data and results as presented, rather than just incorporating conclusions from the studies themselves. In that sense, these generalizations should primarily be treated as hypotheses. The language and concepts in summaries, while obtained from studies, are standardized.

Relevance clues. Clues studies inevitably involved classification; their results were categories of criteria used by users or factors affecting users in inferences about relevance, including different characteristics of information objects. Classification schemes and category labels more or less differed from study to study. However, the most important aspect of the results is that the studies independently observed a remarkably similar or equivalent set of relevance criteria and clues.

Generalizations:

◊ Criteria used by a variety of users in inferring relevance of information or information objects are finite in number and the number is not large; in general, criteria are quite similar despite differences in users. *Different users* use *similar criteria.*

◊ However, the weight (importance) different users assign to given criteria differs as to tasks, progress in task over time, and class of users. For instance, children assign little or no importance to authority, whereas faculty assigns a lot. *Different users, tasks, progress in tasks, classes of users* use *similar criteria*, but may apply *different weights.*

◊ Although there is no wide consensus, on a general level, clues and associated criteria on which basis users make relevance inferences may be grouped as to:

  □ *Content*: topic, quality, depth, scope, currency, treatment, clarity.

  □ *Object*: characteristics of information objects, e.g., type, organization, representation, format, availability, accessibility, costs.

  □ *Validity*: accuracy of information provided, authority, trustworthiness of sources, verifiability, reliability.

  □ *Usefulness or situational match*: appropriateness to situation, or tasks, usability, urgency; value in use.

  - □ *Cognitive match*: understanding, novelty, mental effort. Link to previous knowledge.

  - □ *Affective match*: emotional responses to information, fun, frustration, uncertainty.

  - □ *Belief match*: personal credence given to information, confidence.

◊ These groups of criteria are *not* independent of each other. People apply multiple criteria in relevance inferences and they are used interactively.

◊ The interaction is between information (or object) characteristics (top three above) and individual (or human) characteristics (bottom four). (In a similar sense this is posited in the Stratified Model, Section 5.2.1.)

◊ Content-oriented criteria seem to be most important for users. However, as pointed out, they interact with others. In other words, criteria related to content, which include topical relevance, are rated highest in importance, but interact with other criteria—they are not the sole criteria.

◊ Criteria used for assigning different ratings (e.g., relevant, partially relevant, not relevant) are substantially (but not completely) similar. However, the weight (could be positive or negative) assigned to given criteria differs depending on the rating—e.g., weight for the same criterion on a document judged relevant differs from the weight of a document judged not relevant. *Different ratings of relevance* use *similar criteria* but may apply *different weights*.

  - □ Similarly, although the criteria are similar, the importance of criteria changes from the presentation of document representations to the presentation of full text. Some become more important, some less—no clear pattern has emerged. Of all document representations (excluding full text), titles and abstracts seem to produce the most clues.

Dynamics. Ultimately, dynamic studies involved observing changes over time, even though time itself was not involved directly in any of the studies as a variable. Some things indeed change over time, while others stay relatively constant.

Generalizations:

◊ For a given task, it seems that the users' inferences about specific information or information object are dependent on the stage of the task.

◊ However, users' criteria for inferences are fairly stable. As the time and the work on the task progress, users change criteria for relevance inferences, but not that much. The users' selection of given information or information objects changes—there is a difference. In addition, the weight given to different criteria may change over stages of work. *Different selections* are made in *different stages* using *similar criteria*, but possibly with *different weights*.

◊ As time progresses and a task becomes more focused, it seems that the discriminatory power for relevance selection increases. *Increased focus* results in *increased discrimination* and *more stringent relevance inferences*.

◊ As to criteria, user perception of topicality seems still to be the major criterion, but clearly not the only one in relevance inferences. However, *what is topical changes with progress in time and task*.

Relevance feedback. Human feedback studies inevitably involved IR systems and search results; however, generalizations here concentrate on how people behaved in relation to relevance feedback:

◊ Human relevance feedback involves several manifestations in addition to commonly used search term feedback, including content, magnitude, and tactics feedback.

◊ Users seem to be more satisfied with systems in which they can incorporate their relevance feedback; when they use relevance feedback, retrieval performance increases. This is valid for laboratory systems and conditions. *Use of relevance feedback* results in *increase in performance*.

    ▫ However, when relevance feedback is available in real life systems and conditions, users tend to use relevance feedback very sparingly—*relevance feedback is not used that much*.

◊ Searching behavior using relevance feedback is significantly different than when not using it as reflected in relevance assessments, selection of documents, time used, and ways of interaction.

    ▫ However, criteria used in relevance feedback are similar to (or even a subset of) criteria used in relevance inferences in general.

CHAPTER 7

Experimental Studies on Effects of Relevance

"If the facts don't fit the theory, change the facts."
Albert Einstein (1879–1955)

7.1 INTRODUCTION

What influences are related to relevance judges and judgments?

It works both ways: Relevance is affected by a host of factors and, in turn, it affects a host of factors as well. A number of studies addressed questions about effects or variables concerning relevance judges and judgments. Of course, factors in these categories are interdependent, as is everything with relevance.

As in the preceding chapter, I will concentrate *exclusively* on observational, empirical, or experimental studies, that is, on works that contained data directly addressing relevance. Works that discuss or review the same topics but do not contain data are *not* included, with a few exceptions in order to provide context. Where appropriate, some summaries include numerical results. Main results from all studies, with a number of caveats, are synthesized and generalized at the end of the chapter.

7.2 RELEVANCE JUDGES

What factors inherent in relevance judges make a difference in relevance inferences?

A similar question was investigated in relation to a number of information-related activities, such as indexing and searching. Not many studies addressed the question in relation to relevance, and those that did concentrated on a limited number of factors, mostly involving the effects of expertise:

➢ Gluck (1995, 1996) used 82 subjects (13 high-school students, three with associate's degrees, 41 with or working on bachelor's degrees, 19 with or working on master's degrees, and 6 with or working on Ph.D. degrees) to (i) respond to an unspecified set of geography-related questions using two packets of geographic materials and (ii) recall their recent experience where geographic questions were raised with responses coded by two coders on a five-point relevance scale in order to study the effects of geographic competence and experience on relevance inferences (1995 study) and compare user relevance and satisfaction ratings (1996 study).

> Dong et al. (2005) asked a physician (whose assessment was considered the "gold standard"), 6 evaluators with biology or medical backgrounds, and 6 without such backgrounds to assess for relevance 132 web documents retrieved by a meta-crawler in relation to specific medical topics in order to measure variation in relevance assessments due to their domain knowledge and develop a measure of Relevance Similarity.

> Hansen and Karlgen (2005) used 8 students and 20 professionals with a variety of academic backgrounds whose first language was Swedish and who were fluent in English to search a newspaper database according to several simulated scenarios serving as queries with results presented in Swedish and English in order investigate how judges assess the relevance of retrieved documents in a foreign language, and how different scenarios affect assessments.

> Ruthven et al. (2007) examined how different aspects of an assessor's context—knowledge of and interest in a search topic, and confidence in assessing relevance for a topic—affect the relevance judgments made. The study was part of the TREC HARD (High Accuracy Retrieval from Documents) track. A number of news test collections and 50 search topics were selected for investigation. Searching was done by participant groups (not further identified as to composition or numbers) that carried out an initial, baseline run and answered a specially constructed form that consisted of questionnaires on assessor's topic familiarity, interest, and confidence, and were presented with a series of document surrogates used in judging. Findings indicated that the 3 factors (interest, knowledge, and confidence) had an effect on how many documents were assessed as relevant and the balance between how many documents were marked as marginally or highly relevant.

7.3   RELEVANCE JUDGMENTS

What factors affect relevance judgments?

A short answer: a lot of them. In a comprehensive review of relevance literature, Schamber (1994) extracted 80 relevance factors grouped into 6 categories, as identified in various studies. She displayed them in a table. In another table, Harter (1996) extracted 24 factors from a study by Park (1993) and grouped them in 4 categories. A different approach is taken here. Rather than extracting still another table, I summarize various studies that tried to pinpoint some or other factor affecting relevance judgments organized on the basis of assumptions made in IR evaluations. The goal is not to prove or disprove the assumptions, but to systematize a wide variety of research questions for which some data has been obtained.

When it comes to relevance judgments, the central assumption in any and all IR evaluations using Cranfield and derivative approaches, including Text Retrieval Conference (TREC)[15] (defined in Section 2.3), has five postulates assuming that relevance is:

1. *Topical*: The relation between a query and an information object is based solely on a topicality match.

2. *Binary*: Retrieved objects are dichotomous, either relevant or not relevant—even if there was a finer gradation, relevance judgments can be collapsed into a dichotomy. It implies that all relevant objects are equally relevant and all non-relevant ones are equally non-relevant.

3. *Independent*: Each object can be judged independently of any other; documents can be judged independently of other documents or of the order of presentations.

4. *Stable*: Relevance judgments do not change over time; they are not dynamic. They do not change as cognitive, situational, or other factors change.

5. *Consistent*: Relevance judgments are consistent; there is no inter- or intra-variation in relevance assessments among judges. Even if there is, it does not matter; there is no appreciable effect in ranking performance.

These are very restrictive postulates, based on a highly simplified view of relevance—not at all following the reality of how people actually judge relevance in real life. The postulates are stringent laboratory assumptions, easily challenged. In most, if not all, laboratory investigations in science things are idealized and simplified in order to be controlled; IR evaluation followed that path. As mentioned, already in 1996, in a scathing criticism of such assumptions about relevance in IR evaluation, supported by empirical data from a number of studies, Harter (1996) pointed out that this view of relevance does not take into account a host of situational and cognitive factors that enter into relevance assessments and that, in turn, produce significant individual and group disagreements. That should be considered—on the one hand. On the other hand, however, using this "weak" view of relevance over decades, IR tests were highly successful in a sense that they produced numerous advanced IR procedures and systems. By any measure, IR systems today are much, much better and more diverse than those of some decades ago. IR evaluation, with or despite of its weak view of relevance, played a significant role in that achievement.

Harter was not the only critic; the debate has a long history. These postulates produced no end of criticism or questioning of the application of relevance in IR tests from both the system and

[15] http://trec.nist.gov/

user point of view. This book is not concerned with IR systems, including their evaluation, thus the arguments are not revisited here. However, the postulates also served as research questions for a number of experimental or observational studies that investigated a variety of related aspects. These are synthesized here, organized along the five postulates.

7.3.1   BEYOND TOPICAL

Do people infer relevance based on topicality only?

This question is treated in Section 3.3.3, and so will not be repeated. It is brought up here because it is one of the postulates in the central assumption for IR evaluation. The short answer is: it seems not. Topicality plays an important, but not at all an exclusive, role in relevance inferences by people. A number of other factors, as enumerated in the section mentioned above, enter as well. They interact with topicality as judgments are made. To answer the question at the top of this section: *No, people do not infer relevance based on topicality alone.*

Here are four additional studies that confirm this conclusion:

> ➤ Xu and Chen (2006) provided 132 undergraduate and graduate students with a choice to select one of four topics and do a Web search that resulted in 262 documents to study relevance judgment criteria as to scope, novelty, topicality, reliability, and understandability. They identified topicality and novelty as the most significant criteria for relevance judgment followed by understandability.

> ➤ Chu (2011) used 2007 Legal TREC to identify factors that affect relevance judgments and those that are more influential. Nine participants (doctoral students in information studies) first conducted searches on a given topic and then submitted up to 100 top retrieved results ranked on a 3-point scale (1 for relevant, 0.5 for somewhat relevant, and 0 for irrelevant) to a legal professional (a graduate assistant with a JD degree) for the next relevance assessment. Those that had been judged as relevant in this round were then submitted to the TREC 2007 Legal Track assessors for final relevance judgment. Findings indicated that there are 11 relevance factors that were selected by 5 or more participants of this study. Specificity/amount of information was ranked the highest, ease of use second highest, and subject matter the third highest, whereas order of presentation was ranked the lowest.

> ➤ Crystal and Greenberg (2006) used twelve participants (students and professionals) recruited from the university and local community to search the Web on a number of health issues in order to observe relevance criteria they used in their searches. Participants were instructed to highlight useful information for each document in the first page of search results. Afterward a think-aloud interview was

conducted. Analysis of the highlights in the searches and contents of think-aloud recordings was done to answer a series of research questions. Findings indicate that relevance judgments of Web users are complex and multifaceted, drawing on a range of document criteria and locations; the most frequently identified criteria were topical ones, but these did not constitute even a majority of identified criteria.

➢   Reichenbacher et al. (2016) used 416 participants as users in a crowdsourcing experiment in order to evaluate effectiveness and validity of 2 methods for assessing geographic relevance (GR) of geographic entities in a mobile use context that include 5 criteria: topicality, spatiotemporal proximity, directionality, cluster, and colocation. Major fin digs: geographic relevance expresses multifaceted relationships between a mobile user's geographic information needs and the geographic entities in the user's environment. The 2 main criteria defining the strength of the GR relationship are the spatiotemporal accessibility of an entity with respect to a user's mobility (spatiotemporal proximity), and the topicality of an entity's affordances with respect to the information need for a particular activity. Furthermore, the strength of the GR relationship is strongly influenced by the geographic context of a user's location, such as spatial clusters and colocation of other relevant geographic entities.

7.3.2   BEYOND BINARY

Are relevance inferences binary, i.e., relevant—not relevant? If not, what gradation do people use in inferences about relevance of information or information objects?

The binary premise was immediately dismissed based on everyday experience. Thus, investigators went on to study the distribution of relevance inferences and the possibility of classifying inferences along some regions of relevance:

➢   Eisenberg and Hue (1987) used 78 graduate and undergraduate students to judge 15 documents in relation to a stated information problem on a continuous 100 mm line in order to study the distribution of judgments and observe whether the participants perceived the break point between relevant and non-relevant at the midpoint of the scale.

➢   Eisenberg (1988) used 12 academic subjects (unnamed whether students or faculty) with "real" information needs to judge the relevance of retrieved "document descriptions" to that need (quotes in the original) in order to examine the application of magnitude estimation (an open-ended scaling technique) for measuring relevance and to compare the use of magnitude scales with the use of category scales.

➢ Janes (1991a) replicated the Eisenberg and Hue (1987) study by using 35 faculty, staff and doctoral students (not distinguished as to numbers) to judge the relevance of retrieved document sets in response to their real information need in order to determine the distribution of judgments on a continuous scale.

➢ Su (1992) used 30 graduate students, 9 faculty and one staff as end users with real questions for which online searches were done by 6 intermediaries. She had the users indicate the success of retrieval using 20 measures in 4 groups in order to determine whether a single measure or a group of measures reflecting various relevance criteria is the best indicator of successful retrieval.

➢ Janes (1993) rearranged relevance judgment data from 2 older studies (Rees and Schultz, 1967 and Cuadra et al., 1967) and from 2 of his own studies with 39 faculty and doctoral students used in the first study and 33 students and 15 librarians in the second, along the scales they used in the studies in order to investigate the distribution of relevance judgments.

➢ Tang et al. (1999) report on a study involving 111 undergraduates in psychology that were provided with 10 research topics to choose a topic of interest; then the investigators did a bibliographic search that included documents that were relevant, not relevant, or ambiguous (not identifying on who did it and how) and presented each student with 30 results related to the chosen topic in order to identify the optimal number of relevance categories at which participants indicated having the greatest amount of confidence in their relevance judgments. A 7-point scale was identified as the scale for which participants expressed the highest level of confidence.

➢ Greisdorf and Spink (2001) used 36 graduate students in 3 studies, who in 57 searches related to their personal or academic information need, retrieved 1,295 documents. The students were asked to indicate relevance assessments using various scales and criteria in order to investigate the frequency distribution of relevance assessments when more than binary judgment is used.

➢ Spink and Greisdorf (2001) used 21 graduate students who, in 43 searches related to their academic information need, retrieved 1,059 documents. The students were asked to indicate relevance assessments using various scales and criteria in order to investigate the distribution of relevance assessments along various regions of relevance—low, middle, and high end of judgments as to relevance.

➢ Greisdorf (2003) used 32 graduate students who, in 54 searches related to their personal or academic information needs, retrieved 1,432 documents in response. The students were asked to assess their results using a number of relevance criteria on a continuous relevance scale in order to study the users' evaluation as related to different regions of relevance.

> Turpin et al. (2015) investigated the use of magnitude estimation for judging the relevance of documents and compared it to 2 other sets of relevance judgments: first, the original binary judgments and second, same documents re-judged by a group of 6 master's students on a 4-level ordinal relevance scale. ("Magnitude estimation is a psychophysical technique for the construction of measurement scales for the intensity of sensations," ibid., p. 565). A set of 18 topics of search tasks and documents and their binary relevance judgments from the TREC-8 ad hoc collection of newswire documents was used as the base. Participants (all students, number not given) were used to obtain magnitude estimation. Findings: Magnitude estimation scores were consistent with classical ordinal scores, both on single topics and overall on the 18 aggregated topics; ordering agreement between magnitude estimation judgments and ordinal judgments was higher than between ordinal and binary judgments; it is likely that using a classical scale one would get a similar agreement level.

7.3.3   BEYOND INDEPENDENCE

When presented for relevance judging, are information objects assessed independently of each other? Does the order or size of the presentation affect relevance judgments?

The independence question also has a long history of concern in relevance scholarship. In a theoretical, mathematical treatment of relevance as a measure, Goffman (1964) postulated that relevance assessments of documents depend on what was seen and judged previously, showing that, in order for relevance to satisfy mathematical properties of a measure, the relationship between a document and a query is necessary but not sufficient to determine relevance; the documents' relationship to each other has to be considered as well.

Several papers discussing the issue followed, but only at the end of 1980s did the question start receiving experimental treatment:

> Eisenberg and Barry (1988) conducted 2 experiments, first with 42 graduate students, and then with 32. The subjects were provided with a query and 15 document descriptions as answers ranked in 2 orders: either high-to-low relevance or low-to-high relevance. Each subject was given 1 of the orders, using in the first experiment a category rating scale, and in the second, a magnitude rating in order to study whether the order of document presentation influences relevance scores assigned to these documents. Rank order did have an effect. Participants, who were presented with the

documents ranking from high to low, had a tendency to underestimate the relevance of the individual documents. The opposite tendency appeared when the test participants were presented with the documents ranking from low to high.

➢   Purgaillis and Johnson (1990) provided approximately (their description) 40 computer science students who had queries related to class assignments with retrieved document citations that were randomly "shuffled" for relevance evaluation in order to study whether there is an order presentation bias.

➢   Janes (1991b) asked 40 faculty and doctoral students (numbers for each group not given) with real information requests to judge the relevance of answers after online searches by intermediaries. Answers were given in different formats (title, abstract, indexing) in order to examine how users' relevance judgments of document representation change as more information about documents is revealed to them.

➢   Huang and Wang (2004) asked 19 undergraduate and 29 graduate students to rate the relevance of a set of 80 documents to a topic presented in a random order in the first phase and then sets of 5 to 75 documents presented from high to low and low-to-high relevance in the second phase in order to examine the influence of the order and size of document presentation on relevance judgments. No order effect was visible when fewer than 15 documents were being assessed. A significant indication of order effect was seen when sets of 15 and 30 documents were judged. The indication was still present when sets of 45 and 60 documents were judged, although not in a significant way. When dealing with a set of 75 documents, the order effect is no longer visible.

➢   Xu and Wang (2008) investigated in 2 phases the effect of order in which documents for relevance judgments were presented. In the first phase, 81 paid participants—undergraduate students—were presented with search tasks related to health. They searched 620 documents and judged retrieved documents on an 8-point scale; the order of documents was determined by participants' scores. In the second phase, 94 participants were presented with 264 documents evaluated by at least 1 participant in the first phase. A search engine randomly assigned 44 documents out of the set of 264 to each participant before the start of search. Findings indicated that there was a curvilinear pattern of order effect for a search task of overlapping and related information needs. In a retrieved document list, the perceived relevance of a document depends on its position in a list.

7.3.4   BEYOND STABILITY

Are relevance judgments stable as tasks and other aspects change? Do relevance infer-
ences and criteria change over time for the same user and task, and if so how?

The question is treated in Section 6.3, under relevance dynamics, and so will not be repeated. Short
answer: Relevance judgments are not completely stable; they change over time as tasks progress
from one stage to another and as learning advances. What was relevant then may not necessarily
be relevant now and vice versa. In that respect Plato was right: Everything is flux. However, criteria
for judging relevance are fairly stable.

7.3.5   BEYOND CONSISTENCY

Are relevance judgments consistent among judges or group of judges?

Many critics of IR evaluation or of any relevance application had a ball with this question, pointing
out easily observed inconsistencies. However, human judgments about anything related to information are not consistent in general, and relevance judgments are no exception. Why should they be?

As mentioned in Section 2.3, the great-granddaddy of all studies that put some data to the
question and opened a Pandora's box was done at the very dawn of IR development in the 1950s.
Gull (1956), in a study that is also a classic example of the law of unintended consequences, showed
not only that relevance inferences differ significantly among groups of judges, but also inadvertently
uncovered a whole range of issues that IR evaluation struggles with to this day. Actually, consistency
of relevance judgments was not the purpose of the study at all. IR evaluation was. Two groups of
judges judged independently the relevance of 15,000 documents; the agreement between 2 groups
of judges was 30.9%.

Over time, a significant number of relevance consistency studies were done, because this is
an important, even critical, question. Here are most, if not all, of them:

> ➤ Resnick and Savage (1964) in the first relevance consistency study on record,
> used 46 technical professionals to assess the relevance of 34 technical reports and
> patent disclosures to indicate which of these are relevant to their interests in order
> to observe intra-consistency of relevance judgments. The judges were divided into
> four groups each receiving a different representation—full text, citation, and abstract,
> including citation and title. The experiment was repeated after 1 month. Respectively,
> intra-relevance agreements on judgments were for full documents 54%, for citations
> 70%, for abstracts 61%, and for titles 63%.

> ➤ Rees and Schultz (1967) used a total of 153 judges divided in seven groups (as
> listed below) that were given 16 documents in diabetes related to a real research proj-
> ect to judge the relevance of the documents to each of 3 research stages in order to,

among others, observe the inter-consistency of relevance judgments by each group. Respectively, inter-relevance agreement for 21 medical librarians—searchers was 44%, 21 medical librarians—non-searchers was 40%, 14 medical experts—researchers was 58%, 14 medical experts—non-researchers was 56%, 29 scientists was 55%, 25 residents was 51%, and 29 medical students was 50%.

➢   Cuadra and Katter (1967) used 230 seniors and graduate students in psychology (with different levels of experience) to rate relevance of each of 9 psychology journal abstracts against each of 8 short information requirement statements in order, among others, to observe the degree of inter-judge agreement in relevance ratings as related to the level of training of the judges in the field. Four levels of experience were established. The inter-judge correlations for the 4 experience levels from lowest to highest were .41, .41, .49, and .44.

➢   Saracevic and Kantor (1988) used 5 professional searchers each to search 40 questions, posed by 40 users (19 faculty, 15 graduate students, and 6 from industry) with real information needs. Their pooled results were presented to the users for relevance assessment in order to observe the overlap in retrieval of relevant documents among different searchers. They found that the overlap in retrieval of relevant documents among the 5 searchers was 18%.

➢   Haynes et al. (1990) did not intend to study consistency, but rather to assess MEDLINE use in a clinical setting. However, their report does include data from which consistency rates can be derived. They used 47 attending physicians and 110 trainees who retrieved 5,307 citations for 280 searches related to their clinical problem, and assessed the relevance of the retrieved citations. Authors then used 2 other search groups of 13 physicians experienced in searching and 3 librarians to replicate 78 of those searches where relevance was judged by a physician with clinical expertise in the topic area in order to compare retrieval of relevant citations according to expertise. For the replicated searches, all searcher groups retrieved some relevant articles, but only 53 of the 1,525 relevant articles (3.5%) were retrieved by all 3 search groups. This is the only real-life study on the question.

➢   Shaw et al. (1991) used 4 judges to assess the relevance of 1,239 documents in the cystic fibrosis collection to 100 queries. Judged documents were divided into 4 sets: (A) from query author/researcher on the subject, (B) from 9 other researchers, (C) from 4 postdoctoral fellows, and (D) from 1 medical bibliographer, in order to enable performance evaluations of different IR representations and techniques using any or all of the judgment sets. The overall agreement between judgment sets was 40%.

➤   Janes and McKinney (1992) used a previous study (Janes, 1991) from which they selected relevance assessments by 4 students as users with information requests. The students judged 2 sets of retrieved documents that differed in the amount of information presented (primary judges) and then used 4 undergraduate students without and 4 graduate students with searching expertise (secondary judges) to re-judge the 2 sets in order to compare changes in judgments due to increase in provided information between primary and secondary judges. The overlap in judgment of relevant documents (calculated here as sensitivity) between all secondary judges and primary judges was 68%.

➤   Janes (1994) used 13 students inexperienced in searching, 20 experienced student searchers, and 15 librarians to re-judge 20 documents in each of 2 topics that were previously judged as to relevance by users in order to compare users' versus non-users' relevance judgments. The overall agreement in ratings between original users' judgments and judgments of the 3 groups was 57% and 72% for the respective document sets.

➤   Sormunen (2002) used 9 master's students to reassess 5,271 documents already judged on relevance in 38 topics in TREC-7 and 8 on a graded 4-point scale (as opposed to a binary scale used in TREC) in order to compare the distribution of agreement on relevance judgment between original TREC and newly reassessed documents and seek resolution in cases of disagreement. He found that 25% of documents rated relevant in TREC were rated not relevant by the new assessors; 36% of those relevant in TREC were marginally relevant; and 1% of documents rated not relevant in TREC were rated relevant.

➤   Vakkari and Sormunen (2004) used 26 students to search 4 TREC-9 topics that already had pre-assigned relevance ratings by TREC assessors on a system that provided interactive relevance feedback capabilities, in order to study the consistency of user identification of relevant documents as pre-defined by TREC and possible differences in retrieval of relevant and non-relevant documents. They found that the student users identified 45% of items judged relevant by TREC assessors.

➤   Scholer et al. (2011) examined 6 TREC collections (covering over 8 years of TREC) with binary relevance judgments and 2 with trinary (highly relevant, partially relevant, and not relevant) in order to determine how accurately different assessors judge the relevance of duplicate documents, i.e., intra-assessors consistency was measured. To identify pairs of highly similar documents (considered as duplicate) a straightforward document similarity approach was used. Results show that 15 to 19% of binary judgments and 19 to 24% in trinary were inconsistent.

➤   Ruthven (2014) conducted 3 separate case studies from TREC data (not elaborated as to size); in the first to examine whether assessors' characteristics lead to different relevance assessments; in the second to examine the consistency of expansion term selection; and in the third to study whether the nature of the documents being assessed leads to different relevance decisions (number of assessors not stated). In the first study, he found, among others, that the strongest predictor variable was the participants' declared specific knowledge on the topic before assessing any returned documents. In the second study he found, among others, that the rate of acceptance between the assessors varies significantly, indicating that some assessors are more consistent than others in which terms they see as important. In the third study, he found, among others, that the strongest contributors to the outcome were the percentage of documents assessed as being partially relevant.

➤   Bailey et al. (2015) analyzed 7,971 responses from 98 workers (left undefined) in searching of 180 topics from 3 TREC tracks that were used to derive information need statements ("backstories"), and then search 2 different retrieval systems for each query in order to observe user variability and impact of widely differing queries that searchers construct for the same information need description. They demonstrated that query variability among individuals leads to substantial changes across a range of standard relevance measures, and the effect of this source of variability is substantially more than that arising from topic or system effects.

➤   Zhitomirsky-Geffet et al. (2015) used 35 information science students to rank and assign relevance scores to the same set of search results 3 times, with a few weeks between each round in order to investigate whether and why users change their preferences when assessing search engine results over time. After finishing the rounds of ranking, the subjects were then exposed to the differences in their judgments and were asked to explain them. The findings were that all subjects judged the vast majority of the results differently in every round. However, there was less change in relevance judgments than in rankings. The analysis revealed that the main factors that caused these changes were due to categorical thinking, influence of the learned information, and environmental and emotional factors.

Consistency in relevance judgments (in terms of percentage) was also mentioned in 4 of 7 studies that asked the question: *How does inconsistency in human relevance judgments affect results of IR evaluation?* (reviewed in Section 8.3). The results were: Lesk and Salton (1968) 40%; Burgin (1992) 40%; Wallis and Thome (1996) 48%; and Voorhees (2000) 33%.

7.4   EYE-TRACKING AND BRAIN IMAGING EXPERIMENTS

> *Eye tracking is the measurement of eye activity. Where do we look? What do we ignore?*
> *When do we blink? How does the pupil react to different stimuli?*

Eye tracking locates and follows electronically a person's gaze. Various technologies have been developed for eye tracking—some involve attachments to the eye, while others rely on images of the eye taken without any physical contact. The concept is basic, but the process and interpretation can be quite complex. Beyond the analysis of visual attention, eye data can be examined to measure the cognitive state and workload of a participant.

For decades, eye tracking was applied in a great many different fields and for many purposes, e.g., in reading research, advertising and marketing research, developmental psychology, and much more. Since the last decade, eye tracking was also applied in information science: first in human information behavior studies in general, and more recently in relevance studies, in particular.

Brain imaging or neuroimaging is the use of various techniques to view activity within the human brain. *How do we picture the structure or function of the nervous system in the brain in response to different stimuli?* Brain imaging methods allow neuroscientists and others to see inside the living brain. These methods help us to understand the relationships between specific areas of the brain and what function they serve. Much of this advance in knowledge is the result of technological advances in brain imaging. Basic technologies for brain imaging are: EEG (ElectroEncephaloGraphy); CAT (or CT) (Computerized Axial Tomography) scans; PET (Positron Emission Tomography) scans; and MRI and fMRI (Magnetic Resonance Imaging) (functional Magnetic Resonance Imaging). New technologies (together with new abbreviations) are constantly appearing.

Brain imaging revolutionized neuroscience and affected a number of other fields and applications. A number of techniques are available to investigate the question of how and where in the brain particular perceptual and cognitive processes occur. Tasks or tests can be devised that place varying levels of demand on the cognitive, sensory, or motor capacities of a participant. Performance of these tasks is then correlated with physiological measurements; based on these results, we may go on to ascribe given functions to areas of the brain.

More recently, information science began using neuroscience. Cognitive task-dependent changes, such as assessing relevance judgments of relevant and non-relevant documents, are observed in the brain. Here is a sample of studies involving eye tracking and brain imaging techniques in studies of relevance:

> Balatsoukas, and Ruthven (2012) examined the relationship between use of relevance criteria and visual behavior in respect to predictive relevance judgments. Research design involved observation of participants' eye movements, talk-aloud protocols, and post-search interviews. The results came from the analysis of 281 relevance judgments made by 24 university students, both undergraduates and postgraduates; all participants searched the Web for a real information need. The observation of participants' eye movements during the process of predictive relevance judgment showed that the use of relevance criteria is dynamic and is associated with ranking order, surrogate components (title, summary, and URL), and participants' relevance judgments (very relevant, partially relevant, not relevant). Figure 7.1 shows a participant's eye movement captured with an eye-tracking device.

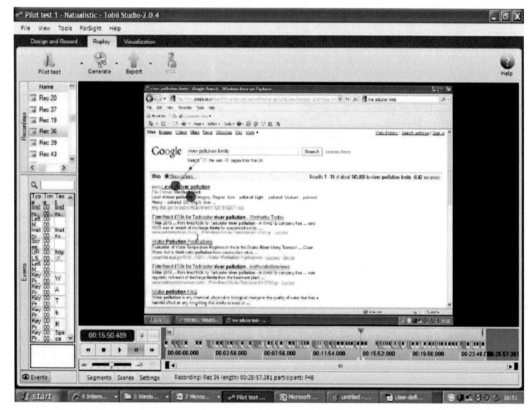

Figure 7.1: A participant's eye movement captured through the use of an eye-tracking device (Tobii T60). From Balatsoukas and Ruthven, 2012.

> Gwidzka (2014) aimed at a better understanding of cognitive processing of text documents at different degrees of relevance. He examined gaze-based metrics in

relation to individual word processing and reading text documents in the context of constricted information search tasks. The findings indicate that text document processing depends on document relevance and on the user-perceived relevance. Most eyetracking-based measures indicated that cognitive effort was highest for partially relevant documents and lowest for irrelevant documents. However, pupil dilation indicates cognitive effort to be higher for relevant than partially relevant documents. Classification of selected eye-tracking measures showed that an accuracy of 70–75% can be achieved for predicting binary relevance. Figure 7.2 shows a difference in eye tracking of documents of different relevance assessment.

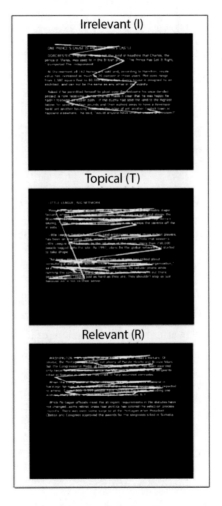

Figure 7.2: Eye tracking of documents with different relevance assessment. From Gwidzka, 2014.

> ➢ Eugster et al. (2014) used Term-Relevance Prediction from Brain Signals (TRPB) to automatically detect relevance of text information directly from brain signals. An experiment with forty participants was conducted to record neural activity of participants while providing relevance judgments to text stimuli for a given topic. Relevance was also associated with brain activity with significant changes in certain brain areas. They showed that detecting relevance from brain signals is possible and allows the acquisition of relevance judgments without a need to observe any other user interaction.

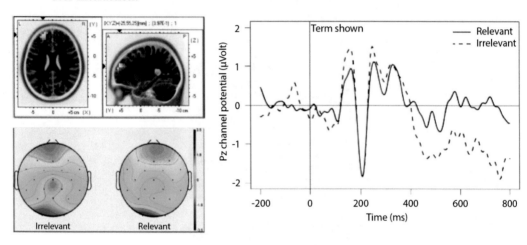

Figure 7.3: Visualizations of physiological findings based on all participants. From Eugster et al., 2014.

> ➢ Gwizdka and Zhang (2015) investigated differences in how 32 users view relevant and irrelevant Web pages on their visits and revisits. Eye-tracking measures were used, with a particular attention paid to changes in pupil size. Users conducted assigned information search tasks on Wikipedia. Findings demonstrate differences in eye-tracking measures on visits and revisits to relevant and irrelevant pages and thus indicate a feasibility of predicting perceived Web document relevance from eye-tracking data. In particular, relative changes in pupil size differed significantly in almost all conditions.

> ➢ Allegretti et al.'s (2015) objective was to identify the time when relevance assessment happens in the brain. Twenty participants from a university assessed the relevance of 100 images (stimuli), 50 relevant and 50 non-relevant, in order to identify the time frame in which the users' brain EEG (electroencephalography) signals are the strongest and most distinguishable from the time that the images are shown

to them. The researchers analyzed how relevance assessment evolves over different windows of time within the first 800 millisecond (ms) of relevance judgment. Timing and topography suggest a time course of processing relevance that involves an early stage in the time window of 180–300 ms and a later stage that begins around 300 ms and builds through 800 ms. This first stage was evident in the larger potentials for relevant images found at frontal and posterior electrode sites.

Eye tracking and brain imaging have a history of many applications. By the second decade of the millennium, relevance research started to join eye tracking and brain imaging research.

7.4.1   SYNTHESIS: RELEVANCE EFFECTS

Caveats abound again and for the same reasons mentioned in the synthesis of the previous chapter (Section 6.5). While similar or even identical research questions were asked in a number of studies, the criteria and methodologies differed so widely that general conclusions offered below are no more than possible hypotheses.

Judges

A very limited number of factors related to relevance judges were studied. This is in sharp contrasts to a much larger number of factors studied in various studies of indexers and searchers (e.g., Saracevic and Kantor, 1988).

◊ Subject expertise seems to be one variable that accounts strongly for differences in relevance inferences by group of judges—*higher expertise = higher agreement, fewer differences.*

◊ Lesser subject expertise seems to lead to more lenient and relatively higher relevance ratings—*lesser expertise = more leniency in judgment.*

◊ Relevance assessment of documents in a foreign language (for native speakers who are fluent in that language) is more time consuming and taxing. Assessment agreement among judges across languages differs; it is lower when assessing foreign language documents.

Judgments

◊ Relevance is measurable—this is probably the most important general conclusion from all the studies containing data.

◊ None of the five postulates in the central assumption of IR testing holds.

▫ However, using these postulates (representing a simplified or weak view of relevance) in a laboratory evaluation produced significant improvements in IR techniques.

◊ What is relevant depends on a number of factors, but the artifact of relevance inferences can be expressed by users on a variety of measures.

◊ Users do not use only binary relevance assessments, but infer relevance of information or information objects on a continuum and comparatively.

▫ However, even though relevance assessments are not binary they seem to be bimodal: high peaks at end points of the range (not relevant, relevant) with smaller peaks in the middle range (somewhat not relevant or relevant). The highest peak is on the non-relevant end.

▫ Following that, relevance judgments may be subdivided into regions of low, middle, and high relevance assessments, with middle being the flattest part of the distribution.

◊ Different document formats (title, abstract, index terms, full text) have an effect on relevance inferences. Relevance judgments do change as information is added, such as from titles, to abstracts, to additional representations. Titles seem to be not as important as abstracts and full texts.

◊ The order in which documents are presented to users seems to have an effect.

▫ It seems that documents presented early have a higher probability of being inferred as relevant.

▫ However, when a small number of documents is presented, order does not matter.

◊ Subject expertise affects consistency of relevance judgments. *Higher expertise = higher consistency = more stringent. Lower expertise = lower consistency = more encompassing.*

◊ Different search request scenarios make a difference in the relevance assessment process as to time but seem not to affect the degree of agreement. *Longer scenarios = more time spent in assessment; all scenarios = similar degree of agreement among judges.*

◊ A complex set of individual cognitive, affective, situational and related variables is involved in individual differences. As of now, we know little about them and can only barely account (beyond hypotheses) for sources of variability.

Consistency

◊ A relatively large variability can be expected in relevance inferences by individuals. Individual differences are a, if not *the*, most prominent feature and factor in relevance inferences.

◊ However, the differences are comparable to individual differences in other cognitive processes involving information processing, such as in indexing, classifying, searching, feedback, and so on.

◊ The inter- and intra-consistency or overlap in relevance judgments varies widely from population to population and even from experiment to experiment, making generalizations particularly difficult and tentative.

   ▫ However, it seems that higher expertise and laboratory conditions can produce an overlap in judgments up to 80% or even more. The intersection is large.

   ▫ With lower expertise the overlap drops dramatically. The intersection is small.

   ▫ In general, it seems that the overlap using different populations hovers around 30%.

   ▫ Whatever the overlap between two judges, when a third judge is added it falls, and with each addition of a judge it starts falling dramatically. Each addition of a judge or a group of judges reduces the intersection dramatically.

   ▫ For instance, it seems that the overlap in retrieval of relevant documents by five different professional searchers when searching the same question drops to under 20%, where pair-wise comparisons were much higher.

   ▫ *Higher expertise = larger overlap. Lower expertise = smaller overlap. More judges = less overlap.*

◊ In evaluating different IR systems under laboratory conditions, disagreement among judges seems not to affect, or affects minimally, the results of relative performance among different systems when using *average* performance over topics or queries. The conclusion is counter-intuitive, but a small number of experiments bear it out. So far, evaluators seem right and critics wrong. However, note the use and effects of averaging performance.

▫ Rank order of different IR techniques seems to change minimally, if at all, when relevance judgments of different judges, averaged over topics or queries, are applied as test standards.

▫ However, swaps—changes in ranking—do occur with a relatively low probability. The conclusion of no effect is not universal.

▫ Different judges = same relative performance (on the average).

▫ However, performance ranking over individual queries or topics differs significantly depending on the query.

Measures

◊ Users are capable of using a variety of scales, from categorical to interval, to indicate their inferences.

◊ However, the type of scales or measures used for recording relevance inferences seems to have an effect on the results of measurement. There is no one "best" scale or measure.

◊ It seems that magnitude estimation scales are appropriate for judging relevance; they may be less influenced by potential bias than category scales. However, they are difficult to explain and analyze.

Eye tracking and brain imaging

◊ People gaze, look at documents that they judge as relevant, partially relevant, and not relevant very differently; the shortest gaze is on non-relevant documents.

◊ Brain imaging shows that relevance of text information can be detected directly from brain signals; different brain areas are affected when relevant or non-relevant documents are shown.

CHAPTER 8

Effects of Inconsistent Relevance Judgments on Information Retrieval Test Results

> "There is nothing constant in this world but inconsistency."
> Jonathan Swift (1667–1745)

8.1 INTRODUCTION

What are the effects of inconsistent human relevance judgments on tests of relative performance of different IR algorithms or approaches? Does inconsistency affect test results?

The aim of this chapter is to review studies that contained data (as opposed to discussion only) related to the above questions that are often implied but rarely asked. In the process, I am also providing a historical perspective to these questions and to a general description of IR testing that followed.

8.2 GOLD STANDARD

User relevance (i.e., user judgments of what is relevant) is the gold standard against which system relevance (and with it a system's performance) is measured (Section 2.3). Thus, performance assessment of a given system (or algorithm) is based on, and follows from, human judgments regarding the relevance of information or information objects provided in response to a given query or information need. This is the case in *all* tests of IR systems.

Establishing this gold standard as to what is relevant to a query is one of the main problems, even conundrums, of IR testing. Not surprisingly then, in many reports of IR tests, the critical step showing how relevant information or information objects became relevant is often shrouded in mystery;

- or, it is glossed over;

- or, it is accepted from a previous source without further ado;

- or, some collective group, such as "judges" or "librarians" or "searchers" or "students" is mentioned as bearing the responsibility;

- or, some such explanation;

- in general, it is hard to get at.

8.2.1   METHODS FOR OBTAINING GOLD STANDARDS FOR TESTING

The objective of relevance judgments in IR tests is to get as close as possible to real-life situations, so that test results would have real-life validity. This is very, very difficult to achieve. Thus, various simulation methods were developed. There are four methods by which relevance judgments have been obtained that are regarded as gold standards.

1. *By the user or questioner*—the person who posed their own question made the judgment as well.

2. *By a user surrogate*—such as a specialist (or by consensus of a group of specialists acting together) who performs judgments on the topic of a given question in their own specialty.

3. *By an information professional* (or by consensus of a group of information professionals acting together) who is professionally entrusted or involved with some aspect of the process, and who performs judgments on the topic of a given question that is not necessarily in his/her specialty, but is familiar with what is going on.

4. *By "bystanders"* signifying none of the above—e.g., by students asked to perform a given task of judgment, including possible prescreening.

Only the first method involves "real users" and the others "laboratory-type users." All IR tests that followed used one or more of these methods for establishing gold standards, with the first method used the least because it is the most difficult to secure.

Here are examples from Cranfield tests.

- In Cranfield 1 tests:

  "... the search questions had been obtained from several hundred individuals in 58 different organisations, mainly in England and America. Each question was based on a single document in the test collection, and a search was considered successful if that particular paper was located in the catalogue" (Cleverdon, 1991, p. 4).

  This is a variation of the theme of the second method above. Questions came from an unknown number of individual specialists who were asked to pose a question(s) on the basis of a source document, and the gold standard was the document from which the question came. However, additional documents were retrieved, and the issue became how to deal with them as to relevance. These "were assessed in relation to the appropriate question" (Cleverdon, 1962, p. 52). Presumably, the project members did the additional relevance assessments, thus bringing in the third method.

- In Cranfield 2, the procedure for getting the gold standard was changed: a number of authors of recent research papers (in aeronautics) provided a question based on the problem that led to the research, together with more questions that arose during the conduct of research; the authors also were given a set of references to judge as to their relevance to these questions. Evaluated references comprised the gold standard for each question. This is a combination of the first and second method. However, some prescreening also was done by students, so the fourth, or "bystander," method was used as well.

Generously, the Cranfield collection with relevance assessments was provided as open source for sharing. Subsequently, it was used in many IR tests, including in some SMART tests. With this, Cranfield relevance assessments migrated as well.

Here is a sampling of some other tests:

- SMART test collections used the second and third method (Salton, 1969).

- Saracevic et al. (1988) used the first method.

- Shaw et al. (1991) used the second and third method.

- TREC uses the second method, with some derivative tests using the third and fourth method (Harman, 2011).

Needless to say, all of these tests faced similar difficulties as the Cranfield tests in obtaining gold standards, but subsequently, all abandoned the use of a source document as the standard the way it had been used in the Cranfield 1 tests. In some form or other, sometimes real users but mostly surrogates—specialists, information professionals, or bystanders—were the ultimate relevance judges for gold standards.

On the historical side, it is quite interesting if not even amazing to note that the basic methodological principles and model for testing, including obtaining relevance judgments for gold standard used in comparison, laid down a half century ago, are still governing IR testing today. IR testing is like a river that became broader and deeper but never changed its course. The course seems to be steady.

IR systems, as conceptualized, will never get away from relevance. For people, relevance is here to stay. Thus, it is here to stay with all associated problems for IR systems as well.

8.3   BUT DOES IT MATTER?

How does inconsistency in human relevance judgments affect results of IR evaluation?

The critics of IR evaluation posited, among other things, that because of inconsistency in human relevance judgments, the results of IR evaluations dependent on stated judgments are suspect. Again, Harter (1996):

> "*Researchers conducting experimental work in information retrieval using test collections and relevance assessments* **assume** *that Cranfield-like evaluation models produce meaningful results. But there is massive evidence that suggest the likelihood of the contrary conclusion*" (ibid., p. 43, emphasis in the original).

How do you evaluate something solely based on human judgments that are not stable and consistent? This is a perennial question, even a conundrum, for any and all evaluations based on human decisions that by nature are inconsistent, way above and beyond IR evaluation.

As far as I can determine there are only seven studies that addressed the issue (Harter (1996) reviewed in detail the four published up to that date). Most of them are modeled on the first and often cited Lesk and Salton (1968) study that had actual data on the complaint voiced by critics. Four of the seven studies also had data that show the magnitude (percentage) of agreements on relevance judgments, thus can also be used as data for consistency studies reported in the previous chapter (Section 7.3.5) and that are not repeated there.

> ➢ Lesk and Salton (1968) used 8 students or librarians (not specified as to which) who posed 48 different queries to the SMART system containing a collection of 1,268 abstracts in the field of library and information science, to assess the relevance of those 1,268 documents to their queries (called the A judgments). Then a second, independent set of relevance judgments (B judgments) was obtained by asking each of the 8 judges to assess for relevance 6 additional queries not of his/her own in order to rank system performance obtained using 4 different judgments sets (A, B, their intersection, and union). They found that the overall agreement between original assessors (A) and 8 new assessors (B) was 30% and concluded after testing 3 different IR techniques that all sets of relevance judgments produce stable performance ranking of the three techniques.

> ➢ Cleverdon (1970) reports on re-judging documents from the Cranfield 2 investigation by 3 additional judges, using 42 topics, 19 index languages, and a 5-level relevance scale. Two hundred documents were selected for each topic to focus on documents originally judged relevant, plus some additional documents from the corpus. Each judge re-judged all topics. The rankings of the normalized recall (NR)

scores for the index languages were then compared using Spearman's ρ for each of the 3 new judges in addition to the original Cranfield judges; correlations were found to be at least 0.92 for each combination of judges. Cleverdon concludes, similarly to Lesk and Salton (1968), that performance measures and rank-orders remain similar despite differences in relevance assessments.

➢   Kazhdan (1979) took the findings from the Lesk and Salton (1968) study as a hypothesis and used a collection of 2,600 documents in electrical engineering that had 60 queries with 2 sets of relevance judgments—1 from a single expert and the other from a group of 13 experts—in evaluating 7 different document representations in order to compare the performance of different representations in relation to different judgment sets. He found that Lesk and Salton's hypothesis was confirmed: the relative ranking of the 7 different representations remained the same over 2 sets of judgments; however, there was 1 exception where ranking changed.

➢   Burgin (1992) used a collection of 1,239 documents in the cystic fibrosis collection (Shaw et al., 1991) that had 100 queries with 4 sets of relevance judgments in the evaluation of 6 different document representations in order to compare performance as a function of different document representations and different judgment sets. The overall agreement between judgment sets was 40%. He found that there were no noticeable differences in overall performance averaged over all queries for the 4 judgment sets; however, there were many noticeable differences for individual queries.

➢   Wallis and Thome (1996) used seven queries from the SMART CACM collection of 3,204 computer science documents (titles and in most cases, abstracts) that already had relevance judgments by SMART judges in order to compare 2 retrieval techniques. Then 2 judges (paper authors, called judge 1 and 2) assessed separately 80 pooled top-ranked retrieved documents for each of 7 queries in order to rank system performance using 3 different judgments sets (SMART, intersection, and union of judge 1 and 2). They found that the overall agreement between original assessors (SMART) and 2 new assessors (judge 1 and 2) on relevant documents was 48%. After testing 2 different IR techniques they concluded that the 3 sets of relevance judgments do not produce the same performance ranking of the 2 techniques, but the performance figures for each technique are close to each other in all 3 judgment sets.

➢   Voorhees (2000) (also in Voorhees and Harman, 2005, pp. 44, 68–70) reports on 2 studies involving TREC data. (Reminder: A pool of retrieved documents for each topic in TREC is assessed for relevance by a single assessor, the author of the topic, called here the primary assessor.) In the first study, 2 additional (or secondary) assessors independently re-judged a pool of up to 200 relevant and 200 non-relevant documents as judged so by the primary assessor for each of the 49 topics in TREC-4; then the performance of 33 retrieval techniques was evaluated using 3 sets of judgments (primary, secondary union, and intersection). In the second study, an unspecified number of assessors from a different and independent institution, Waterloo University, judged more than 13,000 documents for relevance related to 50 TREC-6 topics; next, the performance of 74 IR techniques was evaluated using 3 sets of judgments (primary, Waterloo union, and intersection). Both studies were done in order to look at the effect of relevance assessments by different judges on the performance ranking of the different IR techniques tested. Voorhees found that in the first study, the mean overlap between all assessors (primary and secondary) was 30%, and in the second study, 33%. After testing 33 different IR techniques in the first and 74 in the second test, she concluded: "The relative performance of different retrieval strategies is stable despite marked differences in the relevance judgments used to define perfect retrieval" (Voorhees 2000, p. 714). Swaps in ranking did occur but the probability of the swap was relatively small.

➢   Bailey et al. (2008) used 3 classes of judges: 3 "gold standard" judges, who are topic originators and are experts in a particular information seeking task; 1 "silver standard" judge, who is a task expert but did not create topics; and 19 "bronze standard" judges, who are those who did not define topics and are not experts in the task. Documents (numbers not mentioned) from TREC Enterprise 2007 test collection were searched on 33 topics in order to determine if it is sufficient to invalidate the use of a test collection for measuring system performance when relevance assessments have been created by silver standard or bronze standard judges. Analysis showed low levels of agreement in relevance judgments between these 3 groups. Further, they found that task and topical expertise affect relevance judgments in a consistent manner; also, differences in relevance assessments affect performance scores. Overall, they conclude that the Cranfield method of evaluation (on which TREC is also based) is somewhat robust to variations in relevance judgments.

8.4   SYNTHESIS: EFFECT ON IR EVALUATION

Given that relevance judgments are inconsistent, which they are to various degrees, how does this affect results of IR evaluation? This is a serious question for acceptance of results of such evaluations. Here are some generalizations derived from data in seven studies in Section 8.3, and as summarized in Saracevic (2008).

Caveats expressed in the synthesis of Chapters 6 and 7 are valid for these conclusions as well.

◊ In evaluating different IR systems under laboratory conditions, *disagreement among judges seems not to affect or affects minimally the results of relative performance among different systems* when using *average* performance over topics or queries. The conclusion of no effect is counter-intuitive, but a small number of experiments bears it out. However, note that the use of averaging performance affects or even explains this conclusion.

◊ *Rank order* of different IR techniques seems to change minimally, if at all, when relevance judgments of different judges, averaged over topics or queries, are applied as test standards.

◊ However, *swaps*—changes in ranking—do occur with a relatively low probability. The conclusion of no effect is not universal.

◊ Another however—*rank order* of different IR techniques does change when only *highly relevant* documents are considered—this is another (and significant) exception to the overall conclusion of no effect.

◊ Still another however—performance ranking over *individual* queries or topics differs significantly depending on the query.

CHAPTER 9

Conclusions

"The noblest pleasure is the joy of understanding."
Leonardo da Vinci (1452–1519)

9.1 INTRODUCTION

The purpose of this book is to trace the evolution and with it the history of thinking and research on relevance in information science and related fields from the human point of view. The book does *not* deal with the technological and algorithmic point of view, namely, it does *not* address how systems deal with relevance as related to information or information objects. This is done with full recognition that the technological landscape is changing enormously and rapidly.

The objectives are to present the results of this thinking and research in a way that may be useful not only for enhancing a general understanding of the notion of relevance but also, hopefully, for attempts to incorporate some of that understanding in design and operations of information retrieval systems, search engines included.

The conclusions include a discussion of four large issues affecting all kinds of human endeavors, including relevance. Toward the end, the synthesis summarizes the basic questions addressed in relevance research over time, summarizing also the contents of this book.

Finally, at the very end—well, the thought is worth contemplating.

9.2 GLOBALIZATION OF RELEVANCE

The Internet and the Web have become household names—globally. As information retrieval (IR) also went global, relevance went global. Relevance went to masses.

From the very start of information science in the 1950s, both information science and scholarship on relevance was concerned primarily, if not even exclusively, with problems associated with scientific, technical, professional, business, and related information. In a significant way it still is. However, things in the real world changed dramatically—new populations, new concerns entered. With the development of the Web and massive search engines starting in the mid-1990s, and social media in the 2000s, the public, people, also became increasingly concerned with information in every facet of life. *Relevant* information is desired, no matter what the field, what the issue. The rapid, global spread of information searching is nothing short of astonishing. Millions of users perform untold millions of searches every day all over the globe, seeking elusive, relevant information.

The thirst for relevant information is global, massive, and unquenchable. As relevance went global and public, a number of questions emerged.

To what extent are the results of relevance scholarship—primarily concerned, as mentioned, with a restricted and relatively well-defined population and information—are also applicable to the broad public and every conceivable type of information? A great many fascinating questions worthy of research could be asked. Here are but a few.

- *Are relevance clues similar/different?*

- *Is human relevance behavior similar/different?*

- *Can the broad public be defined at all as to relevance effects?*

It seems that the globalization of relevance also has exposed a need for an additional and different agenda and approach for relevance scholarship. These questions have not been addressed yet.

9.3   RELEVANCE AND SOCIAL MEDIA

Social media has exploded. These are websites and applications that focus on building online communities of people who share content, explore interests and activities, collaborate, and participate in networking. Many social media sites have emerged, but few big ones dominate. Information technology (IT) truly diversified and exploded when it entered the realm of social media.

Social media is a people thing, even though a great many institutions, organizations, even governments try to participate. Social media is also a power, used for both good and bad. Freedom of expression is a hallmark of social media, thus often debated, assailed, and defended in various ways. Social media also enhances human connections and changes cultures. Sometimes, it even entices revolutions.

Social media is not one thing—there are all kinds of very different social media used for all kinds of activities: from science and health, to music, pictures, videos, and bookmarking; from commerce, marketing, and selling; to locating, identifying, and mapping; from expressing opinions—commenting, and blogging, to crowdsourced wisdom; from niche-working to ... you name it.

People utilize social media also to find, use, and communicate relevant information. Relevance and social media are very much connected. However, so far there is little or no research addressing the issues involving the two. Similar research questions could be asked, as in the preceding section addressing globalization. Here is a sample.

- *Are relevance clues used in various kinds of social media similar/different from each other? Are they similar/different from clues found in relevance research in the past?*

- *Is human relevance behavior similar/different?*

- *Can the users of social media be defined at all as to relevance effects?*

- *Are there any generational differences in use of social media and subsequent relevance behavior? As the saying goes: is email indeed just for old people?*

We come to the same conclusions as in the preceding section: Social media has exposed a need for an additional and different agenda and approach for relevance scholarship. These questions have not been addressed yet.

9.4 PROPRIETARY RELEVANCE

Increasingly, relevance is becoming proprietary because major search engines are proprietary. IR techniques used by a majority of larger search engines are well known in principle, but proprietary and thus unknown in execution and detail. Algorithms for deriving relevant answers are secret.

From anecdotal evidence, we know that proprietary IR systems are very much interested in relevance and that they conduct their own relevance studies. Results are not disseminated in open literature. There may have been (or not) some major advances in understanding relevance behavior and effects from studies done at proprietary systems. After all, they have developed, or are trying to develop, a number of innovations that include user-in-the-loop techniques. For that, they must have studied users. For the most part, we do not know the results of the studies, even though we may observe innovations as they occur.

Relevance research may be developing into a public branch where results are shared freely and widely, and a proprietary branch in which research results, if any, remain secret. One cannot escape the irony of the situation. The Internet and the Web are hailed as free, universal, and democratic, and their very success is directly derived from the fact that they were indeed free, universal, and democratic. Yet, proprietary relevance research is anything but.

9.5 "INFORMING SYSTEMS DESIGN"

Relevance-oriented user studies became a burgeoning area of research with the following justification formulated a while ago:

> *"By looking at all kinds of criteria users employ in evaluating information, not only can we attain a more concrete understanding of relevance, but we can also inform system design"* (Schamber et al., 1990, p. 773).

"Informing systems design" became a mantra for a majority of relevance studies in particular and a great many human information behavior studies in general. This book is not an exception. In the objectives of this book (Section 1.2), the same intent, the same mantra is expressed.

This seems logical. However, it is not really happening. Why not? The question was analyzed and lamented upon by a number of researchers and commentators about the state-of-affairs in information science, e.g., Ruthven (2005).

Researchers representing the systems viewpoint simply took a stance: "*Tell us what to do and we will do it*." But the user side was not "*telling*" much beyond the mantra. Unfortunately, "*telling*" is not that simple. A lack of a suitable theory (discussed in Section 5.1) is also a contributing factor.

Relevance is a feature of human intelligence. Human intelligence is as elusive to "algorithm-ize" for IR as it was for artificial intelligence (AI) for many decades after its start in the 1950s. Recent AI advances came about after it abandoned such "algorithmization" of intelligence, and its research and practice simply went pragmatic.

Very little was ever done to actually translate results from user studies into system design, as discussed in detail by Ingwersen and Järvelin (2005). In a way, this is not surprising. The problem is exceedingly difficult theoretically and pragmatically.

However, is the problem of incorporating to a sufficient degree users' concerns, characteristics, and the like into systems essentially intractable? In other words, is the optimistic relevance as suggested by the mantra warranted?

I believe that the sentiment beyond the mantra is warranted, but it cannot be realized by the underlying hope that somebody, somehow, somewhere, sometime will actually do it. I believe that systems designs and operations on the one hand, and users on the other, could and should be connected in a much more consequential, involved, and direct way than they are now, where the connection is from minimal to none. More pragmatically, an effort has to be extended toward work that will connect various research findings with practice and demonstrate a change. The fruitfulness of such a connection was proven in a great many fields, repeatedly.

9.6   SYNTHESIS: BASIC QUESTIONS

Here are some basic questions addressed in relevance research over time.

◊ *Nature*: What are the dimensions or attributes of relevance of specific interest to information science? What may be appropriate theoretical or modeling frameworks within which relevance may be considered and which may serve as the base for all other investigations of relevance?

◊ *Manifestation*: What are the differing ways and contexts in which relevance manifests itself? What is an appropriate typology or taxonomy of relevance for use in further clarification and exploration?

◊ *Behavior*: Relevance does not behave, people do. So: How do people behave in respect to relevance? In particular, how do people determine relevance of information or information objects?

◊ *Effects*: What influences are related to relevance? In particular, what are effects or variables related to relevance judgments and judges?

9.7   FINALLY

Information technology, information systems, and information retrieval will change in ways that we cannot even imagine, not only in the long run, but even in the short term. They are changing at an accelerated pace.

However, no matter what, relevance is here to stay. Relevance is timeless. Concerns about relevance will always be timely.

References

Allo P. (2014). Relevant information and relevant questions: Comment on Floridi's "understanding epistemic relevance". *Minds and Machines*, 24(1), 71–83. DOI: 10.1007/s11023-013-9325-3. 25

Allegretti, M., Moshfeghi, Y., Hadjigeorgieva, M., Pollick, F.E., Jose, J.M., and Pasi, G. (2015). When relevance judgement is happening? An EEG-based study. *Proceedings of the 38th International ACM SIGIR Conference on Research and Development in Information Retrieval*, 719–722. DOI: 10.1145/2766462.2767811. 76

Anderson, T.D. (2005). Relevance as process: judgements in the context of scholarly research. *Information Research*, 10(2) paper 226. Retrieved from http://InformationR.net/ir/10-2/paper226.html. 55

Baeza-Yates, R. and Ribiero-Neto, B. (2011). *Modern Information Retrieval: The Concepts and Technology behind Search*. (2nd edition). Boston, MA: Addison Wesley. DOI: 10.1007/s10791-010-9158-0. 32

Bailey, P., Thomas, P., Craswell, N., De Vries, A.P., Soboroff, I., and Yilmaz, E. (2008). Relevance assessment: Are judges exchangeable and does it matter? *Proceedings of the 31st Annual International ACM SIGIR Conference on Research and Development in Information Retrieval*, 667–674. DOI: 10.1145/1390334.1390447. 86

Bailey, P., Moffat, A., Scholer, F., and Thomas, P. (2015). User variability and IR system evaluation. *Proceedings of the 38th International ACM SIGIR Conference on Research and Development in Information Retrieval*, 625–634. DOI: 10.1145/2766462.2767728. 72

Balatsoukas, P. and Ruthven, I. (2012). An eye-tracking approach to the analysis of relevance judgments on the Web: The case of Google search engine. *Journal of the American Society for Information Science and Technology*, 63(9), 1728–1746. DOI: 10.1002/asi.22707. 74

Barry, C. L. (1994). User-defined relevance criteria: An exploratory study. *Journal of the American Society for Information Science and Technology*, 45(3), 149–159. DOI: 10.1002/(SICI)1097-4571(199404)45:3<149::AID-ASI5>3.0.CO;2-J. 51

Barry, C. L., and Schamber, L. (1998). User criteria for relevance evaluation: A cross-situational comparison. *Information Processing & Management*, 34(2-3), 219–236. DOI: 10.1016/S0306-4573(97)00078-2. 51

Barry, C.L. (1998). Document representations and clues to document relevance. *Journal of the American Society for Information Science*, 49(14), 1293–1303. DOI: 10.1002/(SICI)1097-4571(1998)49:14<1293::AID-ASI7>3.0.CO;2-E. 51

Bateman, J. (1998). Changes in relevance criteria: A longitudinal study. *Proceedings of the American Society for Information Science*, 35, 23–32. 55

Belkin, N. J. (2015). People interacting with information. *SIGIR Forum*, 49(2), 13–27. DOI: 10.1145/2888422.2888424. 21, 23, 24, 32

Bilal, D. (2012). Ranking, relevance judgment, and precision of information retrieval on children's queries: evaluation of Google, Yahoo!, Bing, Yahoo! Kids, and Ask Kids. *Journal of the American Society for Information Science* and Technology, 1879–1896. DOI: 10.1002/asi.22675. 53

Brin, S. and Page, L. (1998). The anatomy of a large-scale hypertextual Web search engine. *Computer Networks and ISDN Systems*, 30 (1-7), 107–117. DOI: 10.1016/S0169-7552(98)00110-X.

Borlund, P. (2003). The IIR evaluation model: a framework for evaluation of interactive information retrieval systems. Information Research, 8(3) paper no. 152. Retrieved from http://informationr.net/ir/8-3/paper152.html. 21, 32

Burgin, R. (1992). Variations in relevance judgments and the evaluation of retrieval performance. *Information Processing and Management*, 28(5): 619–627. DOI: 10.1016/0306-4573(92)90031-T. 73, 85

Bush, V. (1945). As we may think. *Atlantic Monthly*, 176(1), 101–108. Retrieved from http://www.theatlantic.com/doc/194507/bush. 8

Choi, Y., and Rasmussen, E. M. (2002). Users' relevance criteria in image retrieval in American history. *Information Processing and Management*, 38 (5), 695–726. DOI: 10.1016/S0306-4573(01)00059-0. 52

Chu, H. (2011). Factors affecting relevance judgment: A report from TREC Legal track. *Journal of Documentation*, 67(2), 264–278. DOI: 10.1108/00220411111109467. 64

Cleverdon, C. W. (1962). Report on the testing and analysis of an investigation into the comparative efficiency of indexing systems. *ASLIB Cranfield Research Project*. UK: Cranfield Institute of Technology. Retrieved from http://sigir.org/resources/museum/. 83

Cleverdon, C. W. (1967). The Cranfield tests on index language devices. *Aslib Proceedings*, 19(6), 173–194. Retrieved from https://www.ischool.utexas.edu/~stratton/rdgs/Cleverdon.pdf. DOI: 10.1108/eb050097. 13

Cleverdon, C. W. (1970). The effect of variations in relevance assessments in comparative experimental tests of index languages. *Cranfield Library Report no. 3*. UK: Cranfield Institute of Technology. Retrieved from http://sigir.org/resources/museum/. 84

Cleverdon, C. W. (1991).The significance of the Cranfield tests on index languages. *Proceedings of the 14th Annual International ACM SIGIR Conference on Research and Development in Information Retrieval*, 1–12. DOI: 10.1145/122860.122861. 13, 82

Chu, H. (2011). Factors affecting relevance judgment: A report from TREC Legal track. *Journal of Documentation*, 67(2), 264–278. DOI: 10.1108/00220411111109467. 64

Cool, C., Belkin, N., and Kantor, P. (1993). Characteristics of texts reflecting relevance judgments. *Proceedings of the 14th Annual National Online Meeting, Medford, NJ: Learned Information*, 77–84. 50, 51

Cosijn, E. and Ingwersen, P. (2000). Dimensions of relevance. *Information Processing and Management*, 36(4), 533–550. DOI: 10.1016/S0306-4573(99)00072-2. 21, 26

Cosijn, E. (2010). Relevance judgments and measurements. In: Bates, M. J. and Maack, M. N. Eds. *Encyclopedia of Library and Information Sciences*, (3rd ed.) New York: Taylor and Francis: 4512–4519. 21

Crystal, A. and Greenberg, J. (2006). Relevance criteria identified by health information users during Web searches. *Journal of the American Society for Information Science and Technology*, 57(10), 1368–1382. DOI: 10.1002/asi.20436. 64

Cuadra, C. A., Katter, R. V., Holmes, E. H., and Wallace, E. M. (1967). *Experimental Studies of Relevance Judgments: Final Report*. 3 vols. Santa Monica, CA: System Development Corporation. Available as technical reports from National Technical Information Service (NTIS):PB-175 518, PB-175 517, PB–175 567. 14, 18, 66

Cuadra, C.A. and Katter, R.V. (1967). Opening the black box of relevance. *Journal of Documentation*, 23 (2), 291–303. DOI: 10.1108/eb026436. 14, 70

Dervin, B. and Nilan, M.S. (1986). Information needs and uses: a conceptual and methodological review. *Annual Review of Information Science and Technology*, 21, 3–33. 38

Dong, P., Loh, M., and Mondry, R. (2005). Relevance similarity: An alternative means to monitor information retrieval systems. *Biomedical Digital Libraries* 2(6). Retrieved from http://www.bio-diglib.com/content/2/1/6. DOI: 10.1186/1742-5581-2-7. 62

Eisenberg, M.B. (1988). Measuring relevance judgments. *Information Processing & Management*, 24(4), 373–389. 65

Eisenberg, M.B. and Barry, C. (1988). Order effects: A study of the possible influence of presentation order on user judgments of document relevance. *Journal of the American Society for Information Science*, 39(5), 293–300. DOI: 10.1002/(SICI)1097-4571(198809)39:5<293::AID-ASI1>3.0.CO;2-I. 67

Eisenberg, M.B. and Hue, X. (1987). Dichotomous relevance judgments and the evaluation of information systems. *Proceedings of the American Society for Information Science*, 24, 66–69. 65, 66

Eugster, M.J.A., Ruotsalo, T., Spapé, M.M., Kosunen, I., Barral, O., Ravaja, N., Jacucci, G., and Kaski, S. (2014). Predicting term-relevance from brain signals. *Proceedings of the 37th Annual International ACM SIGIR Conference on Research and Development in Information Retrieval*, 425–434. DOI: 10.1145/2600428.2609594. 76

Fidel, R. and Crandall, M. (1997). Users' perception of the performance of a filtering system. *Proceedings of the 20th Annual International Conference on Research and Development in Information Retrieval*, 198–205. DOI: 10.1145/278459.258568.   51

Fitzgerald, M.A. and Galloway, C. (2001). Relevance judging, evaluation, and decision making in virtual libraries: a descriptive study. *Journal of the American Society for Information Science and Technology*, 52(12), 989–1010. DOI: 10.1002/asi.1152. 52

Ford. N. (2015). *Introduction to Information Behaviour*. London: Facet Publishing. 49

Garcia-Molina, H., Georgia Koutrika, G., and Parameswaran, A. (2011). Information seeking: Convergence of search, recommendations, and advertising. *Communications of the ACM*. 54(11), 121–130. DOI: 10.1145/2018396.2018423. 1

Gluck, M. (1995).Understanding performance in information systems: Blending relevance and competence. *Journal of the American Society for Information Science*, 46(6), 446–460. DOI: 10.1002/(SICI)1097-4571(199507)46:6<446::AID-ASI4>3.0.CO;2-6. 61

Gluck, M. (1996). Exploring the relationship between user satisfaction and relevance in information systems. *Information Processing and Management*,32(1), 89–104. DOI: 10.1016/0306-4573(95)00031-B. 61

Goffman, W. (1964). On relevance as a measure. *Information Storage and Retrieval*, 2(3), 201–203.

Greisdorf, H. (2003). Relevance thresholds: A multi-stage predictive model of how users evaluate information. *Information Processing & Management*, 39(3), 403–423. DOI: 10.1016/S0306-4573(02)00032-8. 66

Greisdorf, H. and Spink A. (2001). Median measure: An approach to IR systems evaluation. *Information Processing and Management*, 37(6), 843–857. DOI: 10.1016/S0306-4573(00)00064-9. 66

Gull, C.D. (1956). Seven years of work on the organization of materials in special library. *American Documentation*, 7(4), 320–329. DOI: 10.1002/asi.5090070408. 12, 69

Gwizdka, J. (2014). Characterizing Relevance with Eyetracking Measures. *Proceedings of the 5th Information Interaction in Context Conference* (New York, NY), 58–67. 74, 75

Gwizdka, J. and Zhang, Y. (2015). Differences in eye-tracking measures between visits and re-visits to relevant and irrelevant Web pages. *Proceedings of the 38th International ACM SIGIR Conference on Research and Development in Information Retrieval*, 811-814. DOI: 10.1145/2766462.2767795. 76

Hansen, P. and Kalgren. J. (2005). Effects of foreign language and task scenario on relevance assessment. *Journal of Documentation*, 61(5), 623–639. DOI: 10.1108/00220410510625831. 62

Harman, D. (2011). Information retrieval evaluation. Morgan & Claypoole, *Synthesis Lectures on Information Concepts, Retrieval, and Services*, Vol. 3, No. 2. DOI: 10.2200/S00368ED-1V01Y201105ICR019. 13, 31, 83

Harter, S. P. (1992). Psychological relevance and information science. *Journal of the American Society for Information Science*, 53(4), 257–270. DOI: 10.1002/(sici)1097-4571(199210)43:9<602::aid-asi3>3.0.co;2-q. 23, 44

Harter, S. P. (1996). Variations in relevance assessments and the measurement of retrieval effectiveness. *Journal of the American Society for Information Science*, 47(1), 37–49. DOI: 10.1002/(SICI)1097-4571(199601)47:1<37::AID-ASI4>3.0.CO;2-3. 62, 63, 84

Haynes, B.R., McKibbon, A., Walker, C.Y., Ryan, N., Fitzgerald, D., and Ramsden, M.F. (1990). Online access to MEDLINE in clinical setting. *Annals of Internal Medicine*, 112(1), 78–84. DOI: 10.7326/0003-4819-112-1-78. 70

Hersh, W. (1994). Relevance and retrieval evaluation: perspectives from medicine. *Journal of the American Society for Information Science*, 45(3), 201–206. DOI: 10.1002/(SICI)1097-4571(199404)45:3<201::AID-ASI9>3.0.CO;2-W. 23

Hirsh, S.G. (1999). Children's relevance criteria and information seeking on electronic resources. *Journal of the American Society for Information Science*, 50(14), 1265–1283. DOI: 10.1002/(SICI)1097-4571(1999)50:14<1265::AID-ASI2>3.3.CO;2-5. 52

Hjørland, B. (2010). The foundation of the concept of relevance. *Journal of the American Society for Information Science and Technology*, 61(2), 217–237. 22

Howard, D. L. (1994). Pertinence as reflected in personal constructs. *Journal of the American Society for Information Science*, 45(3), 172–185. DOI: 10.1002/(SICI)1097-4571(199404)45:3<172::AID-ASI7>3.0.CO;2-V. 51

Huang, X. and Soergel, D. (2013). Relevance: An improved framework for explicating the notion. *Journal of the American Society for Information Science and Technology*, 64(1):18–35. DOI: 10.1002/asi.22811. 22

Huang, M. and Wang, H. (2004). The influence of document presentation order and number of documents judged on users' judgments of relevance. *Journal of American Society for Information Science and Technology*, 55(11), 970–979. DOI: 10.1002/asi.20047. 68

Ingwersen, P. and Järvelin, K. (2005). *The Turn: Integration of Information Seeking and Retrieval in Context*. Berlin, Germany:Springer. 21, 36, 37, 38, 39, 92

International Federation of Library Association and Institutions (IFLA) (1998). *Functional Requirements for Bibliographic Records—Final Report*. Retrieved from: http://www.ifla.org/VII/s13/frbr/frbr1.htm#2.1. 10

Janes, J. W. (1991a). The binary nature of continuous relevance judgments: A study of users' perceptions. *Journal of the American Society for Information Science*, 42(10), 754–756. DOI: 10.1002/(SICI)1097-4571(199112)42:10<754::AID-ASI9>3.0.CO;2-C. 66, 71

Janes, J.W. (1991b). Relevance judgments and the incremental presentation of document representation. *Information Processing & Management*, 27(6), 629–646. DOI: 10.1016/0306-4573(91)90004-6. 68

Janes, J.W. (1993). On the distribution of relevance judgments. *Proceedings of the American Society for Information Science*, 30, 104–114. 66

Janes, J. W. (1994). Other people's judgments: A comparison of users' and others' judgments of document relevance, topicality, and utility. *Journal of the American Society for Information Science*, 45(3), 160–171. DOI: 10.1002/(SICI)1097-4571(199404)45:3<160::AID-ASI6>3.0.CO;2-4. 71

Janes, J.W. and McKinney, R. (1992). Relevance judgments of actual users and secondary users: A comparative study. *Library Quarterly*, 62(2), 150–168. DOI: 10.1086/602442. 71

Jansen, B.J., Spink, A. ,and Saracevic, T. (2000). Real life, real users, and real needs: A study and anlysis of user queries on the web. *Information Processing & Management*, 36(2), 207–227. DOI: 10.1016/S0306-4573(99)00056-4. 56

Ju, B. and Gluck, M. (2011). Calibrating information users' views on relevance: A social representations approach. *Journal of Information Science*, 37(4), 429–438. DOI: 10.1177/0165551511412030.

Kazhdan, T.V. (1979). Effects of subjective expert evaluation of relevance on the performance parameters of document-based information retrieval system. *Nauchno-Tekhnicheskaya Informatsiya*, Seriya 2,(13), 21–24. 85

Kelly, D. (2005). Implicit feedback: Using behavior to infer relevance. In: Spink, A. and Cole, C. (Eds.) *New Directions in Cognitive Information Retrieval.*Berlin, Germany: Springer, 169–186. DOI: 10.1007/1-4020-4014-8_9. 49

Kelly, D. (2006). Measuring online information seeking context, Part 1: Background and method. *Journal of the American Society for Information Science and Technology*, 57(13), 1729–1739. DOI: 10.1002/asi.20483. 35

Kelly, D. (2009). Methods for evaluating interactive information retrieval systems with users. *Foundations and Trends in Information Retrieval*, 3(1-2): 1–224. 32

Kent, A., Berry, M., Leuhrs, F.U., and Perry, J.W. (1955). Machine literature searching VIII. Operational criteria for designing information retrieval systems. *American Documentation*, 6(2), 93–101. DOI: 10.1002/asi.5090060209. 11

Koenemann, J. and Belkin, N.J. (1996). A case for interaction: A study of interactive information retrieval behavior and effectiveness. *Conference on Human Factors in Computing Systems ACM's Special Interest Group on Computer-Human Interaction*; CHI '96. 205–212. DOI: 10.1145/238386.238487. 56

Lesk, M.E. and Salton, G. (1968). Relevance assessment and retrieval system evaluation. *Information Processing & Management*, 4(4), 343–359. DOI: 10.1016/0020-0271(68)90029-6. 73, 84, 85

Maglaughlin, K. L. and Sonnenwald, D. H. (2002). User Perspectives on Relevance Criteria: A Comparison among Relevant, Partially Relevant, and Not-Relevant Judgments. *Journal of the American Society for Information Science and Technology*, 53(5):327–342. DOI: 10.1002/asi.10049. 52

Mizzaro, S. (1997). Relevance: The whole history. *Journal of the American Society for Information Science*, 48(9), 810–832. DOI: 10.1002/(SICI)1097-4571(199709)48:9<810::AID-ASI6>3.0.CO;2-U. 20

Mizzaro, S. (1998). How many relevances in information retrieval? *Interacting with Computers*, 10(3), 303–320. DOI: 10.1016/S0953-5438(98)00012-5. 20

Mooers, C.N. (1951). Zatocoding applied to mechanical organization of knowledge. *American Documentation*, 2(1), 20–32. DOI: 10.1002/asi.5090020107. 10

Park, T. K. (1993). The nature of relevance in information retrieval: An empirical study. *Library Quarterly*, 63(3), 318–351. DOI: 10.1086/602592. 50, 51, 62

Park, T. K. (1994). Toward a theory of user-based relevance: A call for a new paradigm of inquiry. *Journal of the American Society for Information Science*, 45(3), 135–141. DOI: 10.1002/(SICI)1097-4571(199404)45:3<135::AID-ASI3>3.0.CO;2-1. 41

Purgaillis, P.L.M. and Johnson, R.E. (1990). Does order of presentation affect, users' judgment of documents? *Journal of the American Society for Information Science*, 41(7), 493–494. DOI: 10.1002/(SICI)1097-4571(199010)41:7<493::AID-ASI2>3.0.CO;2-0. 68

Quiroga, L.M. and Mostafa, J. (2002). An experiment in building profiles in information filtering: the role of context of user relevance feedback. *Information Processing & Management*, 38(5), 671–694. DOI: 10.1016/S0306-4573(01)00058-9. 56

Rath, G. J., Resnick, A. and Savage, T.R. (1961). Comparison of four types of lexical indicators. *American Documentation*, 12 (2), 126–130. DOI: 10.1002/asi.5090120208. 14

Rees, A.M. and Schultz, D.G. (1967). *A Field Experimental Approach to the Study of Relevance Assessments in Relation to Document Searching*. 2. vols. Cleveland, OH: Western Reserve University, School of Library Science, Center for Documentation and Communication Research. Available as technical reports from National Technical Information Service (NTIS): PB-176 080, PB-176 079. ERIC report numbers: ED027909, ED027910. 14, 66, 69

Reichenbacher, T., De Sabbata, S., Purves, R. S., and Fabrikant, S.I. (2016). Assessing Geographic Relevance for Mobile Search: A Computational Model and Its Validation via Crowdsourcing. *Journal of the Association for Information Science and Technology*. Published online. DOI: 10.1002/asi.23625. 65

Resnick, A. (1961). Relative effectiveness of titles and abstracts for determining relevance of documents. *Science*, 134 (3684), 1004–1006. DOI: 10.1126/science.134.3484.1004. 14

Resnick, A., and Savage, T. R. (1964). The consistency of human judgments of relevance. *American Documentation*, 15(2), 93–95. DOI: 10.1002/asi.5090150206. 69

Robertson, S. (2008). On the history of evaluation in IR. *Journal of Information Science*, 34(4), 439–456. DOI: 10.1177/0165551507086989. 13

Ruthven, I, Lalmas, M., and van Rijsbergen, K. (2003). Incorporating user search behavior into relevance feedback. *Journal of the American Society for Information Science and Technology*, 54(6), 529–549. DOI: 10.1002/asi.10240. 56

Ruthven, I. (2005). Integrating approaches to relevance. In; Spink, A. and Cole, C. (Eds.) *New Directions in Cognitive Information Retrieval*. Berlin, Germany: Springer. 61–80. DOI: 10.1007/1-4020-4014-8_4. 39, 40, 92

Ruthven, I. (2014). Relevance behaviour in TREC. *Journal of Documentation*, 70(6), 1098–1117. DOI: 10.1108/JD-02-2014-0031. 72

Ruthven, I., Baillie, M., and Elsweiler, D. (2007), The relative effects of knowledge, interest and confidence in assessing relevance. *Journal of Documentation*, 63(4),482–504. DOI: 10.1108/00220410710758986. 62

Salton, G. (1969). *Information Storage and Retrieval: Scientific Report No. ISR-7*. (also included are ISR reports 8 through 16). The National Science Foundation. Retrieved from http://sigir. org/resources/museum/. 83

Saracevic, T. (1975). Relevance: A Review of and a framework for the thinking on the notion in information science. *Journal of the American Society for Information Science*, 26(6), 321–343. [considered as Part I. in relation to Saracevic, 2007a,b]. DOI: 10.1002/asi.4630260604. 15, 18

Saracevic, T. (1991). Individual differences in organizing, searching and retrieving information. *Proceedings of the American Society for Information Science*, 28, 82–86.

Saracevic, T. (1996). Relevance reconsidered. *Proceedings of Second International Conference on Conceptions of Library and Information Science*, (CoLIS 1996). Ingewersen, P. and Pors, N. O. (Eds.), Copenhagen: The Royal School of Librarianship. 201–218. 26, 53

Saracevic, T. (1997). The stratified model of information retrieval interaction: Extension and applications. *Proceedings of the American Society for Information Science*, 34, 313–327. 21, 34

Saracevic, T. (1999). Information science. *Journal of the American Society for Information Science*, 50(12), 1051–1063. DOI: 10.1002/(SICI)1097-4571(1999)50:12<1051::AID-ASI2>3.0.CO;2-Z. 7

Saracevic, T. (2007a). Relevance: A review of the literature and a framework for thinking on the notion in information science. Part II: nature and manifestations of relevance. *Journal of the American Society for Information Science and Technology*, 58(3), 1915–1933. DOI: 10.1002/asi.20682. 18, 21, 26, 34

Saracevic, T. (2007b). Relevance: A review of the literature and a framework for thinking on the notion in information science. Part III: Behavior and effects of relevance. *Journal of the American Society for Information Science and Technology*, 58(13), 2126–2144. DOI: 10.1002/asi.20681. 15

Saracevic, T. (2008). Effects of inconsistent relevance judgments on information retrieval test results: A historical perspective. *Library Trends*, 56(4), 763–783. DOI: 10.1353/lib.0.0000. 15, 86

Saracevic, T. (2016). Relevance: In search of a theoretical foundation. In: Sonnenwald, D. (ed). *Theory Development in the Information Sciences*. Austin, TX: University of Texas Press.

Saracevic, T. and Kantor, P. (1988). A study of information seeking and retrieving: III. Searchers, searches, and overlap. *Journal of the American Society for Information Science*, 39(3), 197–216. DOI: 10.1002/(SICI)1097-4571(198805)39:3<197::AID-ASI4>3.0.CO;2-A. 70, 77

Saracevic, T., Kantor. P., Chamis, A. Y., and Trivison, D. (1988). A study of information seeking and retrieving. I. Background and methodology. *Journal of the American Society for Information Science*, 39(3), 161-176. DOI: 10.1002/(SICI)1097-4571(198805)39:3<161::AID-ASI2>3.0.CO;2-0. 83

Schamber, L. (1991). User's criteria for evaluation in a multimedia environment. *Proceedings of the American Society for Information Science*, 28, 126–133. 50, 51

Schamber, L. (1994). Relevance and information behavior. *Annual Review of Information Science and Technology*, 29, 3–48. 62

Schamber, L., Eisenberg, M.B., and Nilan, M.S. (1990) A re-examination of relevance: Toward a dynamic, situational definition. *Information Processing & Management*, 26(6), 755–776. DOI: 10.1016/0306-4573(90)90050-C. 32, 50, 91

Schamber, L. and Bateman, J. (1999). Relevance criteria uses and importance: Progress in development of a measurement scale. *Proceedings of the American Society for Information Science*, 33, 381–389. 52

Scholer, F., Turpin, A., and Sanderson, M. (2011), Quantifying test collection quality based on the consistency of relevance judgments. *Proceedings of the 34th International ACM SIGIR Conference on Research and Development in Information Retrieval*, 1063–1072. 71

Schutz, A. (1970). *Reflections on the Problem of Relevance*. New Haven, CT: Yale University Press. 41, 44

Schutz, A. and Luckman, T. (1973). *The Structures of the Life-World*. Evanston, IL: Northwestern University Press. 35, 41

Sedghi, S., Sanderson, M., and Clough, P. (2013). How do healthcare professionals select the medical images they need? *Aslib Proceedings: New Information Perspectives*, 65 (1), 54–72. DOI: 10.1108/00012531311297186. 53

Shaw, W.M. Jr., Wood, J.B., Wood, R.E., and Tibbo, H.R. (1991). The cystic fibrosis database: Content and research opportunities. *Library & Information Science Research*, 13(4), 347–366. 70, 83, 85

Smithson, S. (1994). Information retrieval evaluation in practice: A case study approach. *Information Processing and Management*, 30(2): 205–221. DOI: 10.1016/0306-4573(94)90065-5. 54

Sormunen, E. (2002). Liberal relevance criteria of TREC: Counting on negligible documents? *Proceedings of the 25st Annual International Conference on Research and Development in Information Retrieval of the Special Interest Group on Information Retrieval, Association for Computing Machinery*, 324–330. DOI: 10.1145/564376.564433. 71

Sperber, D. and Wilson, D. (1986). *Relevance: Communication and Cognition.* Cambridge, MA: Blackwell. 43

Sperber, D. and Wilson, D. (1995). *Relevance: Communication and Cognition.* (2nd ed.) Cambridge MA: Blackwell. 43

Spink, A. and Greisdorf, H. (2001). Regions and levels: Measuring and mapping users' relevance judgment. *Journal of the American Society for Information Science*, 52(2), 161–173. DOI: 10.1002/1097-4571(2000)9999:9999<::AID-ASI1564>3.0.CO;2-L. 66

Spink, A. and Saracevic, T. (1997). Human-computer interaction in information retrieval: nature and manifestations of feedback. *Interacting with Computers*, 10(3), 249–267. DOI: 10.1016/S0953-5438(98)00009-5. 56

Su, L.T. (1992). Evaluation measures for interactive information retrieval. *Information Processing & Management*, 28(4), 503–516. DOI: 10.1016/0306-4573(92)90007-M. 66

Swanson, D. R. (1986). Subjective versus objective relevance in bibliographic retrieval systems. The *Library Quarterly*, 56(4), 389–398. DOI: 10.1086/601800. 24

Tang, R., Vevea, J. L., and Shaw, W. M., Jr. (1999). Towards the identification of the optimal number of relevance categories. *Journal of the American Society for Information Science*, 50(3), 254–264. DOI: 10.1002/(SICI)1097-4571(1999)50:3<254::AID-ASI8>3.3.CO;2-P. 66

Tang, R. and Solomon, P. (2001). Use of relevance criteria across stages of document evaluation: On the complementarity of experimental and naturalistic studies. *Journal of the American Society for Information Science*, 52,(8), 676–685. DOI: 10.1002/asi.1116. 55

Taylor, A. (2012). A study of the information search behaviour of the millennial generation. *Information Research*, 17 (1). Retrieved from http://www.informationr.net/ir/17-1/paper508.html. 53

Taylor, A. (2013). Examination of work task and criteria choices for the relevance judgment process. *Journal of Documentation*, 69(4), 523–544. DOI: 10.1108/JD-12-2011-0054. 53

Tombros, A. and Sanderson, M. (1998). Advantages of query biased summaries in information retrieval. *Proceedings of the 21st Annual International Conference on Research and Development in Information Retrieval of the Special Interest Group on Information Retrieval, Association for Computing Machinery (SIGIR 98)*, 2–10. DOI: 10.1145/290941.290947. 51

Toms, E.G., O'Brien, H.L., Kopak, R., and Freund, L. (2005). Searching for relevance in the relevance of search. *Proceedings of Fourth International Conference on Conceptions of Library and Information Science, (CoLIS 2005)*. F. Crestani and I. Ruthven (Eds.). Berlin, Germany: Springer, 59–78. DOI: 10.1007/11495222_7. 52

Turpin, A., Scholer, F., Mizzaro, S., and Maddalena, E. (2015). The benefits of magnitude estimation relevance assessments for information retrieval evaluation. *Proceedings of the 38th International ACM SIGIR Conference on Research and Development in Information Retrieval*, 565–574. DOI: 10.1145/2766462.2767760. 67

Vakkari, P (2001). Changes in search tactics and relevance judgments when preparing a research proposal: A summary of findings of a longitudinal study. *Information Retrieval*, 4(3), 295–310. 55

Vakkari, P. and Hakala, N. (2000). Changes in relevance criteria and problem stages in task performance. *Journal of Documentation*, 56(5), 540–562. DOI: 10.1108/EUM0000000007127. 55

Vakkari, P. and Sormunen, E (2004). The influence of relevance levels on the effectiveness of interactive information retrieval. *Journal of the American Society for Information Science and Technology*, 55(11), 963–969. DOI: 10.1002/asi.20046. 71

van Rijsbergen, C. J. (1979). *Information Retrieval*. London: Butterworths. Retrieved from http://www.dcs.gla.ac.uk/Keith/Preface.html. 31

Vickery, B. C. (1959a). The structure of information retrieval systems. *Proceedings of the International Conference on Scientific Information*. Vol. 2, 1275–1290. Washington, DC: National Academy of Sciences. Retrieved from http://www.nap.edu/books/NI000518/html/1275.html. 19, 20

Vickery, B. C. (1959b). Subject analysis for information retrieval. *Proceedings of the International Conference on Scientific Information*. Vol. 2, 855-866. Washington, DC: National Academy of Sciences. Retrieved from: http://www.nap.edu/books/NI000518/html/855.html. 19, 20

Voorhees, E. M. (2000). Variations in relevance judgments and the measurement of retrieval effectiveness. *Information Processing & Management*, 36(5), 697–716. DOI: 10.1016/S0306-4573(00)00010-8. 73, 85, 86

Voorhees, E. M. and Harman, D. K. (Eds.). (2005). TREC. *Experiment and Evaluation in Information Retrieval*. Cambridge, MA: MIT Press. 13, 85

Wallis, P. and Thom, J. A. (1996). Relevance judgments for assessing recall. *Information Processing & Management*, 32(3), 273–286. DOI: 10.1016/0306-4573(95)00061-5. 73, 85

Wang, P. (1997). The design of document retrieval systems for academic users: implications of studies on users' relevance criteria. *Proceedings of American Society for Information Science.* 34, 162–173. 51

Wang, P. and White, M. D. (1995). Document use during a research project: A longitudinal study. *Proceedings of American Society for Information Science.* 32, 181–188. 54

Watson, C. (2014). An exploratory study of secondary students' judgments of the relevance and reliability of information. *Journal of the Association for Information Science and Technology*, 65(7), 1385–1408. DOI: 10.1002/asi.23067. 54

White, H.D. (2007a). Combining bibliometrics, information retrieval, and Relevance Theory: First examples of a synthesis. *Journal of the American Society for Information Science and Technology*, 58(4), 536–559. DOI: 10.1002/asi.20543. 44, 45

White, H.D. (2007b). Combining bibliometrics, information retrieval, and Relevance Theory: Some implications for information science. *Journal of the American Society for Information Science and Technology*, 58(4), 583–605. DOI: 10.1002/asi.20543. 44, 45

White, H.D. (2010). Relevance in Theory. In: Bates, M. J. and Maack, M. N. Eds. *Encyclopedia of Library and Information Sciences*, (3rd ed.) New York: Taylor and Francis: 4498–4511. 46

White, H.D. and Mc Cain, K.W. (1998). Visualizing a discipline: an author co-citation analysis of information science 1972-1995. *Journal of the American Society for Information Science*, 49(4), 327–355. DOI: 10.1002/(SICI)1097-4571(19980401)49:4<327::AID-ASI4>3.0.CO;2-W. 39

White, M.D. and Wang, P. (1997). A qualitative study of citing behavior: Contributions, criteria, and metalevel documentation concerns. *Library Quarterly*, (67)2, 122–154. DOI: 10.1086/629929. 49

Wilson, T.D. (2000). Human information behavior. *Informing Science* 3(2), 49–56. Retrieved from https://www.ischool.utexas.edu/~i385e/readings/Wilson.pdf. 38

Wilson, D. and Sperber, D. (2004). Relevance theory. In: Ward, G. and Horn, L. (eds.) *Handbook of Pragmatics*. Oxford, UK: Blackwell, 607-632. Also: retrieved from http://www.phon.ucl.ac.uk/home/PUB/WPL/02papers/wilson_sperber.pdf. 43, 44

Xu, Y. and Chen, Z. (2006). Relevance judgment: What do information users consider beyond topicality? *Journal of the American Society For Information Science And Technology*, 57(7), 961–973. DOI: 10.1002/asi.20361. 64

Xu, J and Dong Wang, D. (2008). Order Effect in Relevance Judgment. *Journal of the American Society For Information Science and Technology*, 59(8):1264–1275. DOI: 10.1002/asi.20826. 68

Zhitomirsky-Geffet, M., Bar-Ilan, J., and Levene, M. (2015).How and why do users change their assessment of search results over time? *Proceedings of the American Society for Information Science* and Technology, n.p. DOI: 10.1002/pra2.2015.145052010067. 72

Author Biography

Tefko Saracevic is Distinguished Professor Emeritus at the School of Communication and Information, Rutgers University. He was the president of the American Society for Information Science and received the Society's Award of Merit (the highest award given by the Society). He also received the Gerard Salton Award for Excellence in Research, by the Special Interest Group on Information Retrieval, Association for Computing Machinery (also the highest award given by the Group). As of July 2016, in Scopus (the largest abstract and citation database of scientific journals, books, and conference proceedings), he has received 3,762 citations—excluding self-citations. In Google Scholar (with broader coverage of all kinds of documents in addition to journals) he received 11,778 citations. He is a member of a number of editorial boards. From 1985 to 2008 he was the Editor-in-Chief of *Information Processing & Management*, an international journal. Although retired, he is still active—among others, teaching online courses, writing, and participating in conferences. He has published a number of articles on the topic of relevance in information science—an area of professional lifelong interest.

Printed in the United States
by Baker & Taylor Publisher Services